GHOSTS
OF THE
CANADIAN
NATIONAL
EXHIBITION

GHOSTS
OF THE
CANADIAN
NATIONAL
EXHIBITION

Richard Palmisano

DUNDURN
TORONTO

Editor: Jennifer McKnight
Design: Jennifer Scott
Printer: Webcom

Library and Archives Canada Cataloguing in Publication

Palmisano, Richard
        Ghosts of the Canadian National Exhibition / written by Richard Palmisano.

Issued also in electronic formats.
ISBN 978-1-55488-974-7

        1. Canadian National Exhibition (Toronto, Ont.).   2. Haunted places--Ontario--Toronto.   3. Ghosts--Ontario--Toronto.   I. Title.

BF1472.C3P32 2011   133.1'29713541   C2011-901870-5

1   2   3   4   5   15   14   13   12   11

We acknowledge the support of the **Canada Council for the Arts** and the **Ontario Arts Council** for our publishing program. We also acknowledge the financial support of the **Government of Canada** through the **Canada Book Fund** and **Livres Canada Books**, and the **Government of Ontario** through the **Ontario Book Publishing Tax Credit** and the **Ontario Media Development Corporation**.

Care has been taken to trace the ownership of copyright material used in this book. The author and the publisher welcome any information enabling them to rectify any references or credits in subsequent editions.

J. Kirk Howard, President

Printed and bound in Canada.
www.dundurn.com

MIX
Paper from
responsible sources
FSC® C004071

Dundurn	Gazelle Book Services Limited	Dundurn
3 Church Street, Suite 500	White Cross Mills	2250 Military Road
Toronto, Ontario, Canada	High Town, Lancaster, England	Tonawanda, NY
M5E 1M2	LA1 4XS	U.S.A. 14150

To my wife, Michelle.
Thank you for all your support and hard work,
and for coming out with the team.

Contents

We are transforming faces,
Of hate and love,
Happiness, sadness.
Bright and dull.

Colourful or ashen grey,
Depending on the time.
Different songs.
Same rhyme.

Anchored stable, can be moved.
Screaming, quiet whispers.
Singing, speaking your language.
Yet misunderstood.

Morphing as life jolts ahead,
Returning to the past.
The comedians, thrillers,
Lovers and depressants.
Those memories that last.

Growing smarter every day,
Our appeal is big or small.
Can't draw us close, no ridding us,
We live inside you all.

~Amanda Jobe

EXHIBITION PLACE

December 15, 2010

Exhibition Place, home to the Canadian National Exhibition as well as other trade and consumer shows, is known for its bright lights and laughter. But lurking below the surface are a few well-kept secrets about unexplained happenings that, until now, were primarily known to staff who work the late shift. That the grounds should harbour otherworldly visitors is not much of a surprise. The Horticulture Building was once used as a temporary morgue, the current site of the CNE midway was a bloody battlefield during the War of 1812, and the grounds were once home to two military forts. Then there is the CNE's own long history going back to 1879 – plenty of time and plenty of reasons for an accumulation of "things that go bump in the night."

Staff of the CNE & Exhibition Place Archives thought that the public might find this aspect of the grounds to be of interest, so we prepared an exhibit entitled "CNE After Dark." Featured at the 2009 CNE, the exhibit focused on Exhibition Place buildings known to be haunted. Richard Palmisano visited our exhibit and later contacted us to see if we wished to further explore the nature of the hauntings at Exhibition Place. Thus was born an ongoing relationship between staff of the Archives and Richard and his team.

In the fall of 2009, Richard and his team investigated the Archives and the building in which it is located, the General Services Building. Staff of the Archives, as well as staff of the Security Department (who are also located in the General Services Building) have long known this building to have numerous spirits. Richard and his team were able to confirm this as well as help us understand who was haunting our building and the possible reasons why. By late autumn of 2010, Richard and his team had investigated nearly every building at Exhibition Place. Some buildings are relatively quite; others are not, as will become clear to anyone reading Richard's account of his investigations undertaken at Exhibition Place.

In a sense, confirmation by Richard and his team that the grounds are truly haunted has brought Exhibition Place employees together, believers and non-believers alike. That our grounds are haunted is just another colourful part of the long, long history of the parcel of land known today as Exhibition Place.

Linda Cobon

Manager,
CNE & Exhibition Place Archives

Acknowledgements

I'd like to extend a special thank you to the Board of Governors of Exhibition Place; the Board of Directors of the Canadian National Exhibition Association; Dianne Young, CEO, Exhibition Place; Ed Wiersma, Manager, Security, Exhibition Place; Linda Cobon, Manager, Records and Archives, Exhibition Place; Christina Stewart, Media Archivist, Records and Archives, Exhibition Place; and all the men and women serving with Security Services, Exhibition Place.

I'd also like to thank the talented staff at Dundurn, Toronto Police Services Mounted Unit, the *Toronto Star* archive services, and the City of Toronto Archives.

My thanks go to the team for coming out and putting up with me — I thank each and every one of you for your hard work, your time, and, most importantly, your opinion: Sheryl Popp, Amanda Jobe, Michele Stableford, Darrin LaPointe, Peter Roe, and Amanda Keays.

Thanks to the participants for coming out and placing fresh eyes on our work and for bringing new thoughts and opinions forward: Sarah Angeles, Alex Rondini, Jim Costa, Anna DeSousa, Grant MacPhee, Jennifer Foster, Nathan Moles, and Steve Collie.

Thank you to Jonathan Wallace, Helen Balis, Ron Ilchyna, and Roula Balis for their participation at the cemetery.

To Lester Hickman, Craig Williams, and Anthony Scalisi, thank you for your assistance on special technical projects.

Our greatest thanks go to Oz and Sarah Angeles, Mona Fox, and Tony Aronis for their generous donation of important equipment to the Searcher Group.

Thank you to Elaine Stam, graphic and web designer.

A special thank you to my brother Paul for all the time spent on analyzing our surveillance. This was the biggest job we had ever done, with 304 hours of audio/video footage and an additional 44 hours of just audio.

For assistance with the photos, our thanks go to Records and Archives, Exhibition Place; the City of Toronto Archives; the Metro Toronto Police Museum; Peter S. Dzivy; Paul Palmisano; Peter Roe; and Joanne MacDonald, *Toronto Star* archives. Drawings from the barracks were supplied by Amanda Keays.

This project brought together some of the most talented people I know, and it is their special skills and artistic abilities that made this work possible. Even at the scariest of times it was enjoyable, so to everyone involved, thank you.

The Searcher Group

The main mission of The Searcher Group is twofold: the first is to preserve our history and the history of those who have gone before us, and the second is to assist people who are faced with paranormal phenomena and find it difficult to cope with these situations. The Searcher Group assists by providing education, intervention, or conflict resolution. When dealing with hauntings and the spirit world, there are a great number of unknown factors, which is to be expected when dealing with human personalities and their intentions towards others.

In order to provide the best possible help, we rely heavily on the generosity of various levels of government and property owners who allow us to study and work in historical properties and abandoned buildings to gather data, test theories, and conduct experiments. Without their trust and permission, we would not be able to provide the services that we offer. The Searcher Group never charges for its services and all costs are paid directly by the team members. From time to time, The Searcher Group receives gracious donations from interested individuals to assist in our continued research.

The Searcher Group has a deep sense of community and makes itself available to provide lectures, consultations, and assistance to other groups to raise money for charities. Anyone wishing to contact The Searcher Group or the author may do so by emailing *overshadows@sympatico.ca.*

Please do not send attachments, as emails with attachments will automatically be deleted. Visit The Searcher Group at *www.thesearchergroup.ca.*

Why I Hunt Ghosts

The year was 1965; I was four years old and living in a three-bedroom house built in 1899 in the Dufferin and Bloor area of Toronto.

One night I heard the sound of someone walking in the hall, so I slipped from my bed, crept to the door, and peeked out. My room was at the end of the hall, and I could see down the entire length of it. There was no one there, but I could still hear the footsteps on the wood floor coming closer. I ran to the bed, hurling myself in and tossing the covers up over my head, then I heard a terrifying sound — *scrape, scrape, scrape.* The sound itself wasn't terrifying, but the horror came from knowing exactly what that sound was and where it was coming from. It was a lone wire hanger on a single nail just inside my closet door. Something was in there making it move, and the closet door was right next to my bed. I prayed and wished for the sun to rise and for someone, anyone, to come to my room. That morning, as the sun blazed in my window, I realized I had survived my ordeal. I believe that was the moment I decided to find out what these strange sounds were. I've been searching ever since.

Introduction

It was during the 2009 Canadian National Exhibition (CNE) that I made contact with Linda Cobon and Christina Stewart and asked if I could investigate the ghosts that lurked within the buildings and roamed the grounds. Linda invited me down for a meeting. It was a very exciting prospect and a tremendous opportunity to get a glimpse behind the scenes of such an iconic place. I was about to venture through an important place from my childhood.

When we think of the CNE, memories of bright lights, the taste of cotton candy, the rush of people, and the excitement of the rides fill our minds. I remember when I was a teen, one game barker yelling "Doggie, doggie" over and over on his loudspeaker. I now wonder, *Does anyone ever win that dog?*

But when the lights go down and the people head home, the place takes on a life of its own. The spirits that dwell there from the grounds' long history come out to play and work, and even to scare the occasional employee.

The meeting went great. Linda and Christina were extremely knowledgeable about the history of the grounds and buildings, they were down-to-earth, and I knew they were going to be a pleasure to work with on this project. Linda laid out the ground rules, and the first investigation was arranged.

The workers at Exhibition Place had expressed a feeling of discomfort, as well as a sense of curiosity. What no one was coming right out and saying was that there was real fear here, but all the signs were present. Few wanted to go anywhere in the buildings alone, and there were specific areas to be avoided completely.

This is quite understandable, as the grounds and the buildings are so richly steeped in history that they could be magnificent storehouses of energy. It shouldn't be a surprise that Exhibition Place is haunted, as these grounds have been in continual use since well before the eighteenth century. The land was used by the indigenous population and was later home to a French trading post, Fort Rouillé, in 1750, and then Fort York in 1793. One of the bloodiest battles of the War of 1812 was fought on these grounds. With an extensive history of murders and accidents, there are plenty of reasons for hauntings. The grounds were used as a training centre for Canadian troops during the First and Second World Wars. From great accomplishment to tragedy, there has to be a million stories here waiting to be told.

There may be more than just sad stories that entice spirits to dwell here — it may be the joy and excitement that draws them to stay.

When you look deeply into those who have stayed in this place, you will find strong attachments and an incredible sense of duty and responsibility, as if each person honoured their commitment to the fullest. They carried with them pride and accomplishment for being part of something great — something that will live on beyond them. This is the true spirit of Exhibition Place.

THE WAR OF 1812

One of the bloodiest battles of the War of 1812 took place on April 27, 1813, starting just west of the Exhibition Place grounds. The running battle continued east through the present-day midway to the Western Battery. Just slightly northeast of where the Princes' Gates are today, a magazine exploded and killed twenty British soldiers. The fighting continued on to Fort York. The British tried to regroup and fled north to a ravine, where the military cemetery now possibly lies. Knowing they would lose the fort, the British blew up the magazine stores, sending rocks and shrapnel into the American ranks and killing thirty-eight, including Brigadier-General Zebukon Pike, and wounding 222. Although the Americans suffered huge casualties, they took the town of York by noon.

THE START OF SOMETHING NEW

In the province of Ontario, each city once took a turn at hosting a major agricultural fair, and in 1878 it was Toronto's turn. With over 100,000 visitors that year, local politicians and business owners pressed for an annual summer fair to be held in Toronto. This was a banner year, as Thomas Edison had demonstrated electric light, Madison Square Garden opened in New York, milk was sold in glass bottles for the first time, Canada celebrated its first Thanksgiving, and the gates opened to the first Toronto

Courtesy Exhibition Place Archives

A rare photo of the Princes' Gates under construction in 1926.

Industrial Exhibition on September 3. The exhibition would focus on new developments in agriculture, industry, arts, and sciences. In 1904 the name was changed to the Canadian National Exhibition.

The main entrance to the grounds at Strachan Avenue and Lakeshore Boulevard is quite often misidentified as the Princess Gates; but in fact the magnificent edifice and entryway is actually named the Princes' Gates, after Prince Edward and Prince George, who opened the gates on August 31, 1927.

The gates were built to commemorate Canada's sixtieth anniversary of confederation and were originally going to be named "The Diamond Jubilee of Confederation Gates." Thankfully, Prince Edward and Prince George were visiting Toronto and agreed to open the gates that year. They were then named in the princes' honour.

MEDIUMS

The use of mediums within an investigation is one means of collecting information. No information is ever provided to a medium prior to the investigation, to ensure the validity of what is being reported. Other avenues used to collect information are researching historical data and the use of audio and video surveillance systems. Together, these three methods generally provide us the best picture of what is occurring within a haunted location.

EVP

Throughout this book, there are often references to EVP, which stands for electronic voice phenomena, which means voices and/or sounds captured electronically that are believed to be created by spirits of the dead.

Most audio information collected from surveillance systems is not known at the time of our investigation, but rather days later during analysis of what has been recorded.

GHOSTS AND HISTORY

Each time we study the history of anything — be it an artifact, a building, a patch of ground, or even the life of someone past — we are essentially standing on the edge of a ghost story, for it was those people who went before us that created the piece of history we are about to study. How that history is studied or investigated could quite possibly bring you face to face with the creator of that piece of history. They may remain silent or they could be extremely noisy — either way, it remains their choice and thus greatly depends on whether or not they have something to say to us. As researchers, this is essentially what my team and I do: we listen.

First Investigation

General Services Building
October 2009

Paul, Sarah, Christina, and Me

THE HISTORY

The General Services Building was acquired in 1910 and renovated by the Hydro-Electric Power Commission. On January 3, 1911, approval to build hydroelectric towers was granted, and those hydro towers can still be seen today. The power station began receiving hydroelectric power from Niagara on April 29, 1911, and it was in 1959 that the building was handed over to Exhibition Place. Although the facility still serves as a power substation, upper floors have been added and the building has been extensively modified. A new addition was added onto the existing building's east side in 1959, and it was eventually renamed the General Services Building. It now houses maintenance, carpentry, painters, sign makers, security, and the archives.

The early part of this building's past is lost, as Hydro could not supply any information on who built it, what is was used for, or who Exhibition Place took it over from. It became my personal mission to find that missing past.

It all started with Sir Adam Beck: he was a Conservative MPP, and in 1905 he was appointed as a minister under Premier Sir James P. Whitney. Beck felt that privately owned power stations and electrical grids would not serve the public's needs. Beck convinced Whitney that a board of inquiry should be set up to investigate, and that Beck should lead as

Courtesy Exhibition Place Archives

The Strachan Avenue Hydro-Electric Station, photographed here in 1924, became the General Services Building in 1959.

chair. The inquiry found that a municipally owned hydroelectric system funded by the provincial government would serve the public best.

In 1906 Beck was appointed the first chairman of the new Hydro-electric Power Commission. Later that year, the *Power Commission Act* was established. In 1907 Toronto City Council approved the development and public control of hydroelectric power. Soon after, the government took control of privately owned power stations and converted them to its own use.

Beck was knighted by King George V for his work in promoting electricity and the development of power transmission.

It was after about twenty-five hours of research that I discovered the history of this lost structure. In 1901, sitting on leased land that belonged to the city, was a privately owned power station operated by the Ontario Power and Flats Company, which also had offices at 60 Victoria and 107 Niagara, and was managed by Norton V. Kuhlman. The Industrial Exhibition wanted the land in order to expand the cattle market. However, to break the lease, the city would have to pay $3,000 — a hefty sum in 1901, especially considering it already owned the land, which equated to less than half an acre. Ontario Power and Flats Company held a lease of sixteen years, but this lease became null and void when Sir Adam Beck expropriated the building in 1910.

This new information places the General Services Building as the oldest existing building to be built on the Exhibition grounds, with the exception of Stanley Barracks.

THE SHADOW

Many employees have reported seeing a shadow of a man moving down the hallways of the building, only to disappear into a stairway. This shadow person was seen inside the archives by an employee who had just experienced the ghostly apparitions of a woman and child. The person reported that this shadowy figure hurriedly chased after them as if trying to catch up.

THE INVESTIGATION

Paul, Sarah, and I drove out to the site. We stepped from the vehicle into the cool night air, and the three of us stood there a few minutes looking up at the building. No one knew what to expect at this point, although some of the stories I had heard had put me on guard. I took the liberty of not sharing those stories with my brother or colleague, since I wanted them to remain open to whatever lay beyond those old stone walls. I also wanted to keep the team small, at least in the interim, to better assess the level of activity within the General Services Building.

Christina was waiting for us at the front entrance. She led us past the security control centre and through a protected access door to the third floor. The floors were long and open. You could see from one end of the building to the other without restriction, and rooms of various sizes lined both sides of the hallway. As we walked towards the archive rooms, she pointed out some locations where paranormal activity had been recently witnessed. This included the hall in which we now walked, the bathroom, the sign-production room, and a small gym.

We entered the archive main office, where we placed our equipment temporarily, and then continued on into the depths of the archives. We entered a small hall with a freight elevator to the left. Christina looked at me and stopped. "No one likes that elevator," she said.

"What do you mean?" I asked.

"When you enter you get a heavy feeling. People have heard whistling in there."

I looked at the elevator's steel exterior. The heavy grey doors sat silent, but I was intrigued by the whistling. It would have to wait for now, but I made a mental note that this was definitely something I wanted to explore later on.

We moved on around a tight corner to an open area and secure room. Beyond that were the stacks — several aisles of floor-to-ceiling steel shelving filled with banker's boxes, and an apparatus for old film reels. I stood there for a moment thinking that with all these aisles, it would be a challenge to set up surveillance. I looked at Paul and could see he was already making calculations to solve this problem. Sarah moved to the end of the stacks and entered another room, which also housed information and artifacts from the Exhibition's long history, and ended up next to a small kitchenette. She came back around and found another small room to the left and a narrow set of stairs that went up to a tiny mezzanine area. She grasped the handrail and placed one foot on the first step, paused, looked up into the darkness, and joined the rest of us back in the stacks.

The spaces were large and Paul felt he had found the best vantage points to place our equipment. We set up several audio/video surveillance systems in the archive area: one located down by the kitchenette, looking back towards the office, and one midway down near the stacks, looking back towards the kitchenette. He wanted to cover the area thoroughly, so he suggested we place an automatic still camera facing the stairs and one inside the archives just past the main door. We moved to the hallway and Paul set up a surveillance system in the sign production room.

When the systems were set to record, the four of us retreated to the main office to wait.

Our visit seemed uneventful; we quietly packed the equipment and thanked Christina. As we walked out into the night air, I felt disappointed, having hoped that something paranormal might have happened, some sign that this place was truly haunted. I looked at Paul as he tucked the equipment into the trunk. "Seemed quiet," I said, looking back at the third floor window.

"Yeah, but let's see what the surveillance says."

I just nodded and got into the car.

It took several days for Paul to fully analyze the content of what was recorded. When he called me to set up a meeting, all he would say was "We got some stuff."

I drove out to meet him. What did he mean by "stuff"? Whatever the outcome, I was relieved that we had something.

In the archives, the equipment had captured the sound of someone snapping their fingers immediately after we walked away. As we left the room, whispering started near the back kitchenette and the fluorescent lights dimmed. Off in the distance was the sound of bells ringing. Near the camera by the kitchenette came the sound of a door handle turning, and the fluorescent lights brightened to normal.

There was heavy banging from the kitchenette, then, as it grew quiet, there came a male voice recorded as an EVP (electronic voice phenomena) saying "Jim." Another male EVP came immediately after, saying "Yeah." The lights dimmed and the bells rang again. An EVP of a male called the name "Danny." The bells rang as if in reply. A male with a heavy accent said something that sounded like "How long did it take to make that?" The reply was from a female: "Thirteen years."

Paul had a difficult time determining what exactly was being said because of the accent and couldn't figure out what could possibly take thirteen years to make. After a great deal of analysis, he discovered the real question: "How long were you in Jamaica?"

Afterwards, both audio and video portions of this system went to static.

On camera two, the lights seemed to dim, and there was a low banging near the camera. There was an EVP of a male voice calling out a name that sounded like "Karen." The lights brightened again. A female voice said, "I'm ..." but trailed off, becoming inaudible. A male voice asked "What?" Everything went quiet.

After seventeen minutes, the EVPs started again. A male voice was captured saying "Danny." The bells rang a little louder, seeming closer to our system. Again there was a long quiet period. Then what sounded like the same male voice called out, "Danny ... quit playing around."

The lights dimmed again, and a male voice said "Debra." A female voice said "Yes."

A male voice asked, "Did you eat yet?" Then all activity stopped and it was quiet.

Another male voice was recorded, sounding angry: "Get out of this front ..." which trailed off to inaudible.

A male voice said "Yeah."

Bells rang further away from camera, and a great deal of whispering began, none of which was comprehensible.

The camera detected us returning to the midpoint of the archive room. As we were standing there, unknown to us at the time, the furthest camera recorded a male voice with a heavy accent, saying "They come, come." The voice sounded Eastern European.

Bells rang again and the lights brightened. Laughter was heard down near the kitchenette. The last thing recorded as we shut down the equipment was a male voice saying "Debra, honey."

We discussed the electronic voice phenomena we had captured. It was an extremely exciting prospect to know that the building was in fact haunted. This meant there was work to be done, plans to be made, and a team to assemble. I was amazed at how much was recorded and the fact there seemed to be so many different spirits in one area. I also found myself completely confused about what was on our discs. Nothing at this point made any sense to me, and Paul agreed that there seemed to be too many spirits there. There was no indication that they were tied to the history of this building and its uses. It was possible that the analysis could be premature, but we both felt that they didn't belong.

The next day I contacted Christina and reported what was recorded; she too was stumped. I asked her about the lights dimming and brightening throughout our visit, and she told us that the lights didn't usually do that. There wasn't any equipment running that would cause a surge. There seemed to be a real mystery there, and Paul and I couldn't wait to head back. It was our hope that we would come across something in the future that would help identify who all those spirits were and why they were in the General Services Building.

Second Investigation

General Services Building
October 2009

Paul, Amanda Jobe, Christina, and Me

We had arrived early and Christina came down to meet us, escorting us up to the third floor. We quickly went to work setting up two surveillance cameras in the archive room, very similar to our first visit, as we had found those to be very successful. Paul and Amanda placed three groups of trigger items around the area. East of camera one, a ball and doll were placed on the floor and boxed in by bright green painter's tape. To the west of camera one another ball and doll were also taped off. Christina had reported seeing a child in the stacks area on occasion, and it was our hope that these items would prove tempting for the little girl. On the door handle to the kitchenette Paul placed a set of bells, because of the bells recorded on our first visit.

As we started to leave the archive room, Amanda looked at the equipment to ensure it was in order and saw a long, thin, white shape moving quickly across the screen of the monitor. She turned to look down the length of the room but saw nothing.

THE NIGHT WATCHMAN

Many years ago, a night watchman in the General Services Building had a heart attack while making his rounds, and passed away. To this very day he can be heard checking doors, turning off lights, and making his presence known, as is still the practice for security working in the building. On rare occasions he has been seen wandering the building, offering protection from the other side.

THE BURYING GROUND

Just below the Strachan Avenue bridge lies the old military cemetery, which has been there since 1863. The cemetery is divided into two sections, the north half for Protestants and the south half for Roman Catholics.

The first person to be interred here was Private Walsh, who had been buried in a plot within the present-day Exhibition Place grounds near the Dufferin Gate. It was found that the grounds there were far too wet, and the body had to be moved. Because there is no list of people resting in the cemetery, lists are drawn from grave markers, newspapers, regimental information, and archival records.

It is estimated that there may be two hundred graves within the cemetery, but some believe this estimate is low. The last person buried on the grounds was Private Robert Connell on December 22, 1911.

We placed a third system in the second floor hall facing south. Everything was now recording. The consensus was that we should allow the equipment to do its job, and the best way to do this was for all of us to leave the area. Christina suggested that we might want to walk over to a nearby cemetery. This sounded like an interesting prospect, so the four of us left the floor and headed outside to Strachan Avenue.

On the Strachan Avenue bridge we arrived at the top of a steep stairway that led to the cemetery below. We could see the large area that contains graves surrounded by trees, situated in a deep depression.

The four of us moved down the stairs with care and explored the grounds. Paul and Amanda split up to take photographs of the area, and Christina and I moved to a memorial wall to read some of the tombstones. Amanda took two photos with what appeared to be orbs floating in them. This was strange, because she had taken dozens of photographs in the cemetery, but only these two showed orbs.

The cemetery was a fascinating place — as you stood down in this natural depression, it felt as if time had little meaning, even though the modern city hummed and moved all around. I found it peaceful there, and at the same time it was a little bit unsettling, as I had the distinct feeling that there were many eyes upon me. I suggested that we come back with our medium and do a more in-depth investigation of this cemetery at a future date.

Courtesy Paul Palmisano

Paul captured a photo of a thick white mist moving across several stones. This wasn't apparent to any of us at the time, since there was no mist or fog and the night was clear, cool, and windless.

As we were preparing to leave, Paul felt something on his back, and whatever it was fell to the ground. We were unsure what it could have been — possibly someone trying to get his attention.

The four of us walked back to the building and decided to check the exterior. As we moved to the rear of the building, I again had the eerie feeling of being watched. This feeling was completely different in the cemetery — it felt as if we were not welcome back here.

WALKING INTO THE PAST

When an Exhibition Place employee ventured out for a walk, she found herself surrounded by what appeared to be hundreds of men, women, and children, all looking at her. The image dissipated almost immediately.

In their research, archivists discovered this occurred at what was the location of the Toronto Immigration Depot (1875 to the early 1900s). Here up to 1,500 immigrants were housed at one time as they waited to be relocated out west or to northern Ontario.

I shrugged off the feeling and started taking readings of the immediate area. I noted electromagnetic energy readings in open air of between 7 to 10 milligauss and roving frequencies of 4, 52, and 60 hertz. I was close to the power station, but I was getting these readings at approximately 35 and then 45 feet away. The 4 hertz was unusual, but I have seen this come up in haunted locations.

I put my equipment away, but again it felt as if someone was watching us. We lingered a few more moments then headed to the front of the building.

SURVEILLANCE RESULTS

While we were away from the building, the lights began to pulse on the second floor, then there was a bright flash that actually blinded the camera for a few moments. Bells rang several times and there was the sound of dishes and cups moving in the kitchenette.

A male EVP voice called out "Debra." A few moments later the same male voice asked "Where are you?" There was a long pause and then a female voice said "Here." The sound of heavy footsteps passed the camera, but nothing was visible. A male voice called "Mike," and a different male replied almost immediately, "Yeah." The ceiling lights dimmed. A male voice called "Danny."

After a short pause, the sound of bells could be heard. It was a sound very similar to maracas, not the tinny sound you would normally associate with bells. Then something moved our target bells, which have a distinctive sound. Then the lights brightened again.

We made our way back to the third floor to check the equipment, and everything seemed to be operating correctly. As Paul walked towards camera one, located near the kitchenette, a male voice said "You left the door open." Although Paul did not hear the voice at the time, he said it was scary to be alone in a room and then discover the dead are all around you.

As we waited for Paul, we were startled by the sound of something very heavy being moved at the north end of the hall. Everyone turned to see what was going on, but although we could see the end of the hall a mere fifteen feet away, nothing was there. We could clearly hear the heavy scraping sound of wood on concrete.

Then the stairwell door opened and closed. I hurried down the hall to investigate, expecting to find security doing their rounds. I arrived at the stairway and observed that the door was not completely closed. Christina, Amanda, and Paul arrived, and I pointed out the position of the door. Christina mentioned that it should be locked. I pushed it open and tested the handle on the stair side, finding that it was locked.

I could hear something, but as much as I strained, I could not make out what the sound was — it was more like a vibration. I put on my earphones, turned on my parabolic microphone, and immediately heard salsa music in the stairway. I handed the unit to Amanda and she heard slow, classical violin music. The parabolic was handed to Christina and then to Paul, and they also reported classical music. We could not determine the source.

We secured the door and walked back up the hallway. I resituated the camera in the hall facing north, hoping that whatever had been there would return.

I asked to investigate the basement and Christina reluctantly agreed.

As we walked away, the camera in the hall captured male and female voices talking in whispers, and then the camera was moved slightly from left to right by unseen hands.

Christina had been right about the elevator — we stepped in through its gaping mouth, and as she slid the giant steel doors closed, we all immediately felt a heaviness. Paul looked at me and said, "I feel nauseous."

As we arrived in the basement and stepped from the elevator, we all immediately felt a greater tension, as if we were being watched. The four of us explored the long hallways and approached a fenced-in workshop, where the tension intensified tenfold. I moved in to have a closer look, and Amanda and Paul snapped photographs of the basement. I turned away from the gate and caught the look on Christina's face, which made me pause. It was a look of terror, which immediately put me on the defensive.

"What ... are you okay?" I asked her.

"I'm okay," she said, looking slightly pale and shaken. The rest of the team instinctively moved in around her.

"What is it?"

"Something touched me."

"Where, what?"

"Two hands on my waist, my back."

"Are you sure you are all right?" I asked, looking around.

"I'll be fine."

I took out my pendulum and started to ask questions. Amanda had the parabolic microphone and stepped in closer to us.

"Is there a spirit here?"

The pendulum indicated yes.

I looked at Amanda, whose eyes grew wide. She nodded to me as she heard a male answer in the affirmative.

"Mike, is that you? Are you here?"

The pendulum answered yes, and Amanda heard a man say the same.

"Are you here to tell us something, to protect us?"

The pendulum answered yes, and Amanda heard the man say yes.

Amanda heard two female voices whispering to her right, as if they were arguing, then all communication stopped.

Was I in contact with Michael, a worker who had died in this basement back in 1924? I couldn't be sure. And who were those women and what were they arguing about? I had so many questions and felt we could be close to learning more about who might be haunting this building, but after all that had happened, we were on edge, and I felt the best thing was to change our location.

As we returned to the third floor, I told Amanda to check the gym, a room that had been reported as active but was currently locked. As we arrived, I knocked on the door as she pointed the parabolic towards it. She heard rustling, a clang, and a few heavy footsteps — then all went silent.

Christina and I moved into the archives office. Paul headed down the hall and checked the stairwell door, which was still locked. Amanda moved into the sign-design room to take some photos. As she emerged from the room and started across the hall to join us in the office, a chilling male EVP was recorded calling her Emma, then Amanda.

Immediately there were women's hushed whispers, and then all went quiet.

Amanda stepped into the office. "That room feels busy over there, like something is going on. There is always static, and sometimes I can hear faint voices behind the static."

Just beyond the door, in the stacks, the surveillance system recorded the lights pulsing and a great deal of noise: banging, footsteps, and the sound of a police whistle. Although we were not all that far away, no one heard any of these sounds.

A male voice was recorded, calling "Jim."

Paul joined us and we moved into the archives to start packing up. The ball and doll to the east of camera one had been moved and lay slightly across the tape. As we studied the items, we heard laughter coming from the back of the archive room. We moved off to investigate the sounds, but found nothing.

The last system to be retrieved was the camera in the hall. It had captured something black high up in the air that momentarily blocked out the illuminated exit sign that hangs over the stairwell door, the same door that had earlier caught our attention.

The next day I contacted Michele Stableford, one of my team's mediums, to set up our next visit and to see if she could attend. As I was on the phone, she asked who Mike was.

I never like giving information to my mediums, so I asked her who he might be. She told me I had been talking to him recently and that he and Joseph were in the building.

I was shocked that she would pick these two names out of the air, but I also found it fascinating, since she would have no foreknowledge of these people and their place in the history of this building. Until I had called her, she hadn't even known I was working on a job at Exhibition Place. I was very impressed.

Third Investigation

General Services Building, Stanley Barracks, and Exhibition Place Building
January 2010

Paul, Darrin, Amanda, Michele, Sheryl, Linda, Christina, Steve, and Me

The team arrived at my house, and we loaded the equipment. Since we were way ahead of schedule, we decided to stop along the way for something to eat. I knew of a nice family restaurant not far from my house. The team entered and said hello to the manager. The six of us huddled around a couple of tables pushed together and ordered our food. As we waited, Michele excused herself to the ladies' room. A few minutes later she returned to the table, took her seat, and leaned in to tell us that a man had committed suicide in there, and he was still hanging around. I knew this restaurant well and had never heard of anything ever happening here. After we ate, I went up to speak with the manager. I quietly asked him if anything ever happened in the bathrooms. He looked at me for a moment and asked, "Like what?" He knew I was a ghost investigator, so I explained that my medium was here with us and she said something bad had happened in the washroom.

He shook his head and said, "It was a few years ago. A man came in, ordered a meal, ate it,

WOMAN AND CHILD

It has been reported on many occasions that the spirits of a woman and a little girl roam the General Services Building. The woman has been seen wearing a long dress and large hat, and the small girl seems to be always giggling. Her haunting laughter sometimes echoes throughout the long hallways and makes employees pause.

and paid. He then went into the washroom and hung himself with his belt."

I shook my head. "Thanks, I just had to be sure."

"Why?" he asked.

"He's still there."

When we arrived at the General Services Building, before going inside, the team moved around the back of the building. I was looking for Michele's opinion on any activity she might detect back there.

She said she heard men arguing, fighting. "Someone died here. I don't like it back here."

We proceeded to the main door and climbed the stairs to the third floor, where we met Linda, Christina, and their colleague Steve.

Surveillance equipment was set up on the third floor. One camera was placed in the archive at the rear of the section near the kitchenette.

As we were setting up, Michele and Sheryl were standing near the main door to the archives in the hall. Michele saw a man in dark pants, white shirt, and black tie leaning on the wall at the end of the hallway near the stairs. Sheryl looked but could not see him.

"He has authority here. He just left, down the stairs," Michele reported.

As we finished setting up the camera, Amanda started to experience something strange — her heart started to beat faster and she found it difficult to breathe. Michele and Sheryl entered the rear of the archives, and as Michele stepped through the door, she quickly placed her hand over her heart. "Wow, my heart's pounding!" she said. Amanda nodded. A few moments later the sensation subsided.

Paul, Amanda, and I returned to the hallway and set up two cameras facing in opposite directions. While we were setting up, Sheryl and Michele explored the rear of the archives. Sheryl was drawn to a set of stairs that led up to a small area just above the archive. She intuitively felt that there was someone up there and called Michele over to have a look. Michele wanted to investigate the area but decided to wait until the team had assembled.

Sheryl met up with us in the hallway. I wanted to set up a camera in the basement because of what had occurred with Christina on our last visit. Christina offered to escort us downstairs, so we loaded the equipment onto the freight elevator and began our journey down. I could see by the expression on everyone's faces that their feelings were similar to my own. Later, I would speak to each person individually about the elevator ride; they all shared a feeling of horrible, heavy despair. No one liked to be on this elevator, and that included the staff members who have to use it almost daily.

We placed the camera at one end of a very long corridor that ran the entire length of the building. Sheryl reported sensing a man near a ladder positioned inside a locked cage. Christina explained that the ladder went up to a hydro tower. I checked the image on the infrared camera and everything looked good. I set it to record, and we made our way back upstairs to the third-floor archives.

I met Michele and told her that we would start at the very back of the archives, work our way forward, then spend some time in the basement. As we were walking towards the stacks, Michele jumped back, startled, bumping into Amanda.

"What's wrong?" I asked, grabbing her arm to help steady her.

"Wow, I almost walked into him," she said, looking back down the hallway.

"Who?"

"I'm not sure. A tall man, very distinguished, moustache, balding, very well dressed. He went that way." She pointed back towards the front office.

I looked at Amanda — neither of us had seen anything.

The team gathered and we began our tour of the General Services Building interior, with Michele leading the way. She indicated where the man had come through, pointing towards the door. "He was hunched over."

"I'm hearing running, little footfalls, like children," she said, pausing at the room across from the elevator. "There is a man who stays in here and has a moustache and wears glasses. They are around us whispering. There are three spirit energies in here right now; they run around the stacks, they look through the shelving, they are watching. I'm picking up that man in authority again, he's back.

"Someone is here who had lived here, not just him but the whole family. He had a problem with one of his eyes, half open. He says 'I'm here,'" she added. "The kids are giggling," she told us, then she started to laugh.

While using the parabolic microphone, Amanda heard music playing. She described it as music you would hear on a wind-up trinket box.

Michele stopped next to the stairs leading up to the mezzanine level. "Men are whispering upstairs. The energy from up there is pushing us back. I get a strong smell of aftershave or cologne." As we all moved in closer, a cool breeze pushed past us, and we all smelled the aftershave.

Paul detected whispering on his parabolic microphone.

As we stood there quietly, we all heard a child's cry from the stacks area. The sound was short-lived, and some of the team members were having sensory overload, since we were experiencing activity all around us.

Michele, Darrin, and I went upstairs to the small mezzanine area.

"I get a feeling of a male presence, it's strong up here. I get the initial S of a person who is tied to this place, and I hear William. I don't think he belongs up here. They are trying to deter us from being up here. Things will move up here," Michele reported. It was later revealed that the first archivist, Mr. Thomas Edgar Swabey, used to stay overnight in this space during the planning of past CNE fairs.

We headed back downstairs to the archive, where the rest of the team was waiting.

Paul detected music on his parabolic, and Amanda confirmed that she heard it on her headset as well.

We moved around the corner and entered the kitchen.

Michele walked over to a cold spot. "Things get moved here. I hear things breaking. L something? I don't like this room, it feels like something is always watching, something moving around their legs. They come and go in here."

Linda confirmed that there was often a sense of being watched.

"There are many that come and go, but there are no negative feelings," Michele said.

Michele led us back into the archive section opposite the freight elevator. As we did so, Amanda and Sheryl moved into the stacks section of the archives, where they stood quietly in the furthest aisle. Almost immediately came a shuffling of footsteps crossing the floor, then the sound of cardboard being moved. After a few minutes, Amanda and Sheryl rejoined the team.

"I sense boxes get moved a lot," Michele continued. As if on command, we all heard a box move. Everyone started looking around, feeling uneasy.

"A man has just entered. It looks like he's wearing a flight suit, a jump suit. Captain J-something, I just get the letter *J*. And someone has a massive pain in the leg area. Edward, unsure if that is first or last name, just getting the name Edward." As she was talking, Michele moved closer to one of the boxes. Linda asked if she wanted to examine it.

"Something that is supposed to be in here isn't here. It was to be put in here, but isn't. It has been misplaced. It was taken out for a reason, and not brought back. You'll find it. It has to come back! This box gets opened a lot. There is something missing from this box, there are numbers on it. He is here a lot, he's showing me something is missing. He may have died from cancer. He is friendly, and his wife is too."

"Do you want to open the box?" Linda asked.

"I just heard 'be prepared.'" Michele opened the box.

Staring up at her was Doctor Orr's death mask. Doctor Joseph Orlando Orr (1861–1917) was the general manager of the Exhibition from 1903 until his death from a heart attack in 1917. Death masks are plaster or wax impressions of a deceased person's face, sometimes kept as a memento.

"That's the man with the moustache. He is here a lot, as is his wife. He says he was very handsome." Michele paused. "There is something that is missing that belongs with that box. Oh, he is the one with the knee problem. He is the one I saw. He startled me in the hall. Again, it was something that was supposed to be with that." She indicated the file box.

"There are two photos that are supposed to be in that box. The one of Doctor Orr is there, and the one of his wife is unaccounted for," Linda explained.

"It'll show up," Michele said.

Everyone left the archive area and the doors were secured. We moved out onto the third-floor hallway.

Inside, the archive surveillance recorded some activity. A woman's voice called for Jimmy, and a man's called for Debra. There was a heavy bang directly behind camera one near the kitchenette.

An EVP of a male voice called for Danny, and bells sounded in the distance. A male voice said "Get out," and the bells rang again. It appears that

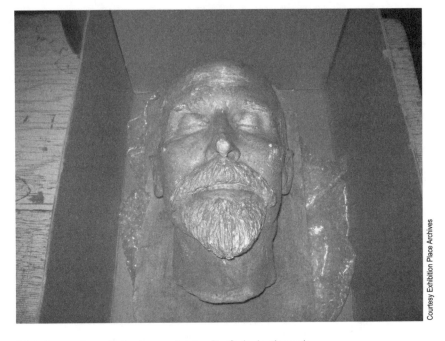

Courtesy Exhibition Place Archives

Michele was drawn to the box containing Dr. Orr's death mask.

Danny is a prankster and can be difficult, and whoever this older male is tries to deal with Danny but becomes extremely frustrated with him.

There was a heavy bang, followed by a louder bang. There was the distinct sound of a door handle turning and a door opening. A small dog's bark was heard. An older male's voice said something, but the content was inaudible. From different directions were sounds of things moving, then all went quiet for a long time.

Finally, there was the sound of a door opening, a short pause, and then a male voice calling out "Help me!" This sounded like a desperate cry.

We moved out into the hallway, and I watched as Michele walked down to the end of the hall. "I just heard a crash of some kind. The man I saw earlier was here, then he went into the stairway," she said, gesturing to a stool against the wall.

Everyone walked back up the hall and entered the sewing room.

"I don't like this room. My head hurts in here. I feel nauseous in here and I smell something burnt. There are a lot of women in here. Men come and go, but the women stay. There is also a man wearing a ball cap who comes in here a lot.

"Someone is crying, an *A* initial, a woman with dark hair. There are so many layers of things in here, a great deal of nausea."

A loud crash was recorded, though not audible to us at the time.

"There is like a secret passage, or doorway, that isn't here anymore. A lot of shadows moving around really quickly," Michele told us as she examined the room.

I pulled the group together. "We should split up and head to the basement. Team One can use the elevator and Team Two can go down the stairs."

Linda agreed.

"I want to go that way, where the man went," Michele said, taking the stairs. "There has been a lot of activity on the stairs. Seems like I'm following him down, like he's leading me."

The team heard talking ahead of them, coming from below, but there was no one there. As we left the floor, surveillance was recording activity.

There was a female EVP calling "Danny." A male EVP yelled "Out." There was a sound like someone pulling tape from a roll then the bells rang again. As we left the hall, a woman's voice began to sing off in the distance.

A male EVP said "Danny." A different male EVP replied "Yes."

Banging started near the camera, getting closer. The camera shifted left, then right. The sound started to cut in and out, and the lens aperture tried to self-adjust, and the lights seemed to brighten and dim. There was no one on the floor, since we had all converged in the basement.

Sheryl again felt dread upon entering the freight elevator. Michele led the way.

"Oh, this area is extremely haunted down here, a lot of energy, lots of smoke. I feel like I have to go in here, but I don't want to. But I have to. There is paint stored here, but not back when I am seeing it. A man walked in. Dark clothing. I hear a dog barking. Stanley? He just walked through the gated area. This is the one place I didn't want to go," Michele reported.

We headed to the cage.

"Oh my god, it just moved," Darrin said, motioning to the cage gate.

"Oh," Michele replied, moving in closer. "There is a really negative person around here, angry. He hates it … don't know why. He is having an argument with someone."

There was banging all around us.

"One-piece jumpsuit, scruffy. He is backing into the corner, into the dark. I keep hearing a dog barking. This area was open at one time, not as closed off. He has dark, curly hair. He says there's more down here than meets the eye. He is gone now. I hear: don't go there, don't go there! I see men building things here, moving parts and motors."

The banging grew louder, and some of the team members were becoming stressed.

"There was a man in there, negative, frustrated, died there. Died there. Like having seizures, I see him having convulsions."

Darrin moved in to get some video of the fenced-in area. He had turned to position his camera when Michele warned him that the spirit down there was angry. As he began to film, the gate was moved by an unseen force and Darrin quickly backed away.

Michele felt that the spirit of this man was trying to get her to turn around, as if it were a warning. She spun around and saw that a sign was posted directly behind her, reading DANGER HIGH VOLTAGE in big red letters.

I saw Sheryl looking towards the caged area, and I asked her to go over and see what she thought. As she neared the cage, she stopped dead in her tracks, raising a hand to her head. "Oh my head hurts. It's like something sharp slashed through my head. It came on so quickly." For some reason she continued moving forward towards the gate and was hit with a feeling she could only describe as like having a convulsion. In a flash she could see nothing except blinding white light. I grabbed her arm to steady her, and she quickly backed away

WORKER DIES AT HYDRO STATION

On October 10, 1924, Michael S., who was employed as a linesman, was electrocuted while working at the Strachan Avenue hydro building (now the General Services Building). Michael had gone to the basement to make repairs from an earlier explosion and fire when he touched a live electrical line with his knee and an iron strap with his head. He was killed instantly.

from the area. The phenomenon immediately ceased. "Oh, what a horrifying feeling that was."

We left the basement and arrived in a newer part of the building, which was built in 1959.

"There is a man and woman that walk through here, up and down this hallway. The woman is more modern, the man goes back further in time. I feel the employees working in here would have negative feelings — that creepy feeling of being watched. Nothing really negative, but because of their era and their connection with this place and the work they used to do here, they are very inquisitive and nosy as to what is being done now, so their energy will be felt by the living, and in that sense will seem like a negative, but I don't see any harm from them," Michele told us.

THE SMELL OF FIRE

It was in February 2009. I was working security with two other members of the security team in the General Services building around two a.m. when we all encountered the smell of burning wood in the south front hallway. The smell was investigated, and it did not seem to extend anywhere beyond this hallway in any direction. It lasted for approximately one half hour. No cause was found.

Reported by an Exhibition Place security officer.

UNDISCLOSED BUILDING, EXHIBITION PLACE GROUNDS

Linda and Christina led us on a tour of another building on the Exhibition Place grounds.

As we entered, Michele said, "There is a man with black pants and a white shirt. He also wears a black tie. He is an authority figure."

We moved down a long open corridor into the main lobby. "There are two men sitting here having a conversation. They are not aware of us at all," Michele stated as she walked over to an empty leather bench.

Amanda detected whispers in the area on the parabolic microphone.

"They have dressier clothing on. They are talking about things that are changing. They are totally oblivious of us being here. You can feel their energy." Michele waved her hand through the air where she perceived them to be.

Several of us saw a shadow move down the hallway and disappear around a corner.

Music was detected in the distance, source unknown.

"I hear hard-heeled shoes or boots. Were there soldiers here at one time?" Michele asked. Footsteps were heard as well as whispering from down the hall.

"Soldiers were stationed here, yes," Linda said.

"They are telling me there is a plaque. Is there a plaque?"

"Yes, out on the front of the building."

"Hold on, there is movement down here." Michele headed off down the hall with us in tow. "Did you hear them say something?" she asked Amanda.

"Yes," Amanda replied, pointing the parabolic microphone.

"They really don't want us in here," Michele told us. She stopped in a large room and looked around. "This is where the music comes from. There is a man who walks around with a suit and tie, very well-to-do, very prestigious. He oversees a lot of what goes on here. He has a very strong connection to this space, like he was the boss." She paused. "I see a mini hospital, or sick bay. A lot of those who were here never came back. They died overseas."

A toilet flushed in the women's washroom as we passed. We entered to investigate and found no one there. The toilets were not equipped with motion or automatic flushing devices, and nothing further was detected.

After a short walk we arrived at Stanley Barracks.

HISTORY

The British Army felt that it was time to replace the aging Fort York, built in 1793, and between 1840 and 1841 the royal engineers constructed the new fort approximately one kilometre west of the original one. There were originally six impressive main buildings constructed of limestone. They surrounded a parade square, and several smaller wooden buildings were later added. This would become Toronto's new garrison and would house 300 men.

In 1870 the British army turned the fort over to the Canadian government, and the site became a training facility for the North-West Mounted Police.

In 1893 the new fort was renamed Stanley Barracks after the governor general, Lord Stanley of Preston. Lord Stanley was the great sports enthusiast who gave us hockey's Stanley Cup.

During the Great War the barracks were used to house German, Austro-Hungarian, and Turkish citizens interned as enemy aliens. During the Second World War, Canadian troops were stationed there, and after the war it was used as emergency housing. By 1951 all the families had been relocated, and by 1953 all of it but the officers' quarters/mess were demolished.

These impressive gates, forged in 1839 in the British Isles, that once stood at the entrance to Stanley Barracks, were sold to a developer and can now been found at the entrance to Guildwood Village in Scarborough.

THE INVESTIGATION

As we stood outside in front of the southwest door, Michele crinkled her nose. "Okay, I'm getting the sense of a morgue, I smell dead people. Not that I sense this building was a morgue, it's just what I am sensing."

Although it wasn't uncommon to store the deceased in a basement during the winter months, due to the ground being frozen, we did not find any evidence of this at the Barracks. If this had been the case, it surely would not have been in the officers' mess.

We entered the building through a heavy door and passed through an iron gate on the stairs.

"This is totally full of energies, a lot of people here. Wow. A fire, lots of smoke. Definitely a feeling of old ladies in this room. A lot of activity, lots of footsteps, floors creaking. Older women, chatting. This was a school at one time, teaching was going on here. There are children running around in here." Michele paused. "Oh, it's cigar smoke, but the smell of dead people is coming up from the basement. So many layers of time and events here. This room was used as a kitchen. Hummm, someone touched my hair, well, the officers were very frisky. The spirits here are aware and intelligent, they will interact. Again, touching me." She was becoming frustrated.

Amanda scanned the area with the parabolic microphone and found a room where she heard wedding music.

Sheryl entered a small space at the end of the hall. It was no bigger than a tiny closet and had recently been cut off from the main room with drywall. As she stepped in, she felt there was something in there with her, and immediately felt that she had to get away. She quickly joined the rest of the group.

Amanda entered another room and heard a deep male voice chanting. She handed the parabolic to Linda, who heard what she believed to be the kind of chanting you would hear in a mosque.

As we moved from room to room, I took photographs of each area.

We ventured down into the basement, where there was a heavy, musky smell. Plaster and paint were peeling from the walls.

On the second floor I took this photo of what appears to be a cat in the window at the top centre of the photo.

Collection of the author

"I still smell death here. I feel there is something below us," Michele said.

Linda indicated that we were in the basement and that there was nothing known to be below that floor.

"There were officers and their families in here, more than that, there are lots of people in here," Michele told us.

An unseen person cleared his throat, and we all heard it.

"Wow, there is high energy in here," Michele said. "Disorienting." She leaned against the doorframe to steady herself. "There is a man with a big moustache. He has a lot of medals, patches on his coat. Sherman. There were four gentlemen who walked past us, two by two."

Several of us felt a cold breeze pass in the hall.

"They turned and vanished down a stairway," she said, pointing to the location. Upon inspection, there was no staircase there. "A male says 'Bye Sam,' whoever Sam is."

We moved upstairs and exited into the night air. Slowly we worked our way back to the General Services Building to retrieve the equipment and call it a night.

We returned to the archives and started to pack up the equipment near the stacks. The camera down near the kitchenette was still recording while we worked. The sound of clapping hands was recorded. A whistle started to sound and a male voice yelled, "Danny." The whistles stopped, and there was whispering in the background. A male voice with a British accent called again for Danny. The dog barked, followed by a loud bang.

There was a heavy tread across the archive floor, like that of a man's hard-soled shoes. This may have been somewhat audible, since both Paul and I looked up from working on the other surveillance system.

The camera recorded us making our way through the stacks towards the sound. The last thing it recorded just before we shut it off was the sound of the bells ringing over and over again and a male voice saying, "Don't talk to me."

Fourth Investigation

General Services Building and Stanley Barracks
January 2010

Paul, Michele, Sheryl, Amanda, Michelle, and Me

We arrived early, and while we waited outside for Linda to meet us, Paul and I discussed where we would place the cameras. I wanted to set up the infrared camera in the basement, but there was no point in placing an audio system down there, since the hum from the electrical vaults was quite loud and would render the audio system useless.

Linda greeted us at the front door and the team headed directly down to the basement. On this visit the cage where a lot of the activity had been focused was found unlocked and wide open. I quickly changed my plans to take advantage of this situation and found a table close by which would be handy to place my equipment on. As several of us positioned the surveillance system in this location, the rest of the team wandered off.

Amanda kept hearing someone walking in the long corridor that runs the entire length of the building, but each time she went to look, nothing was there. She came back to join the rest of us and worked her way closer to the unlocked cage. She felt a sadness in there and told Michele, "It's cold in here!"

A CELEBRATION

On many occasions the Exhibition Place archivist would hear sounds of a party wafting down the hall — men and women talking and laughing, the sounds of glasses clinking together. Any time she ventured out to investigate, the sounds would stop.

Michele nodded.

The system was now up and running, so we decided to leave half the team at the General Services Building, and Paul, Amanda, and I would head over to Stanley Barracks to set up surveillance there. As the three of us left, the rest of the team went up to the archives office to wait.

We met security and drove over to New Fort York. The building was vacant and extremely hot. Dropping our heavy winter coats on the floor near the main door, we quickly went to work setting up.

Back at the General Services Building, the rest of the team settled in to wait for our return. Sheryl inquired if the activity in the archives had increased since our last visit, as our investigations could have stirred things up. (It has been our experience that during investigations, activity normally increases.) Linda said that they hadn't noticed any change in the level of activity.

We placed a camera on the first floor and moved up to the second. I was leading the way, and as I arrived at the top of the stairs, I pushed through the doorway and paused, which made Amanda almost bump into me. A column of light about two inches thick had appeared midway down the hall, coming up out of the floor and touching the ceiling. It lasted about two seconds then was gone. I inspected the area but could find no evidence of it being there. There was no discolouration of the hardwood floor or the ceiling, and static levels appeared normal.

As I set up the system, a great deal of banging could be heard down the hall from one of the rooms east of our position. Paul and Amanda went off to investigate. They returned having found nothing. As Paul assisted me with the camera equipment, Amanda noticed a pool of light on the floor. She walked down to see if it might be some sort of reflection, but the light vanished as she neared it. She showed me the area. It was the same location where I had seen the column of light a few minutes earlier.

The system had failed, and I had to reset the DVR recording system, which normally takes three to four minutes. Paul suggested that instead of standing around waiting, we head to the basement, place the system there, then come back and finish with this unit. So we went downstairs to the basement, and immediately the atmosphere changed to one of thick, heavy, foreboding. Paul told me he felt nauseous.

Amanda detected whispering on the parabolic microphone but could not determine what was being said.

The system was set and operating within a few minutes, but we needed to go upstairs to set the upper floor camera. Paul took the lead, and as he arrived on the second floor he saw a column of light in the same location where Amanda and I had seen it. Paul reported the light had a bluish tinge to it. I set the system to record, and Paul and Amanda looked at the spot. Amanda turned her microphone towards the room next to where they had been standing and said, "I hear music coming from there!" They took several photographs, but nothing further was detected.

The three of us set the alarm and drove back to the General Services Building to join the others.

The team moved back into the depths of the archives, and we let Michele take the lead in an attempt to communicate with the spirits there. Paul and Amanda both had parabolic microphones, and Michele used a digital recorder. Sheryl, Michelle, and I used digital cameras. Linda and Christina observed.

Michele began. "Is there a George here?"

Amanda detected a male voice: "No."

"Can the spirits here come closer?" Michele asked. "Can you give us a clear sign that you are here? Can you touch one of us?"

Sheryl sensed someone was standing in the aisle just behind Michele, so she raised her camera and took a picture. As the flash went off, Michele's hair was pulled hard by an unseen hand that snapped her head back. She cried out in pain and took a moment to recover. "Did you get a shot of that?" she asked.

"I don't think so. I fired just before it happened," Sheryl said.

If this was Michael, then the flash was most likely the cause of what had happened. Since he was killed by electrocution, a flash would undoubtedly translate into horror for him, and possibly even the memory of pain.

"Did you hear anything come up behind me?"

"No, I just felt the whoosh of air."

Regaining her composure, Michele continued. "Can you come close again, please? Sorry I jumped, that hurt. Who am I talking to? Oh, it's

Michael. Why are you sad, Michael? Oh, you were young. Do you like staying here? Then why don't you leave this place?"

Several of us heard weeping from the entrance to the next room. We stood listening quietly.

"Is that you, Michael?" Michele asked.

There was no reply.

"Oh, I'm getting 'George works the grounds.' Whatever that means." Michele laughed. "He says his feet hurt." She paused. "The explosion? There was an explosion here? Slow down! He's talking too fast. Was there an explosion here?"

Linda confirmed that there was.

"Michael wears a hardhat," Michele said. "Who is Daniel? Daniel Smith or Smyth?"

No one had an answer. My wife Michelle heard faint bells from the far end of the room.

Michele kept asking if anyone's knee hurt. "There is a Walter, a soldier. He lost his leg."

An EVP recorded a male voice with a thick Scottish accent saying "Gary." Then all went quiet.

"Don't go. Hello? Come back," Michele said. We waited a moment.

The EVP recorded the same rattle we now associated with Danny.

"Do you like being here? Oh, he does, he is very shy. He likes to follow people around, to see what they are doing. One of you had a cup with a picture on it of a puppy, he likes it very much," Michele stated.

Christina indicated that she did have a mug with a puppy on it that had been broken.

"He is not from here, doesn't belong here," Michele said.

"Did he live nearby?" I asked.

Michele paused for a moment. "Yes."

"Did he live by the bridge?"

"What bridge? There is no bridge."

SOLDIER HIT BY TRAIN

On January 24, 1884, a soldier of the Canadian Rifles was walking along the railway tracks. He stumbled and fell just as a train was passing, and it severed his leg below the knee. He died from his injury soon after. This occurred directly behind the General Services Building.

The bridge I spoke of was the Strachan Avenue bridge, built in the 1880s. All went quiet again. The spirits seemed to fade in and out, so we moved locations.

As the group filed back towards the front office, Sheryl fell behind. As she did she felt a presence directly behind her, so she quickened her pace. Michele, who was now just in front of Sheryl, turned and looked back at her. "He's right behind you," she said.

Sheryl replied, "I know!" They both stopped and tried to get him to talk again, but he ran away.

"They are gone," Michele reported.

One of the great mysteries for investigators of haunted places is that no matter how active a place may be, there are times when all activity ceases completely for several hours or even for a few days. At that time, communication ended in the General Services Building.

We packed up the camera from the basement and moved outside, where the air was fresh and crisp. We decided to let the equipment keep recording at the barracks, and walked over to the military cemetery.

Michele and Sheryl looking for Danny in the archive stacks.

Michele led us down the steep stairs into the graveyard and along the path towards a grassy field beyond the memorial wall. She paused and looked around at the trees that surrounded us. There were men in the trees, five or six of them, watching. There have been reports of people seeing what appeared to be soldiers amongst the trees looking towards the lake.

We stopped in the field, and Michele sensed the presence of a little boy directly beside her. Sheryl put out her hand and felt his energy there. The boy was not wearing a shirt, just pants and suspenders. As Amanda started to walk towards the group, the boy ran to her and asked her where his brother was, but Amanda did not sense him.

Michele started to pick up information, like a flood coming at her all at once. "I see children playing here, layers of time, many layers of time. There is a William Sr., Allen, David." Pointing north, she said, "There is was a mass burial. There is a man standing by the wall post with his arms crossed, and just behind him below the gravel lay bodies."

We decided to end our walk-through at the cemetery for now, first because the temperature was becoming unbearably cold, and second because we needed to get to the Barracks before the recordings were finished.

We walked back to the General Services Building and retrieved our vehicles, then drove to the Barracks. Paul, Amanda, and I went upstairs to retrieve the equipment, while Michele, Michelle, Sheryl, and Christina walked along the first floor and then went to the basement. Sheryl was the first to step into the basement, and she said it felt suffocating, like she was surrounded by people. The smell was horrible, she reported.

Michele took the lead, moving from room to room. "I hear a lot of people talking, men and women. I can't understand what they are saying, but I hear the sounds of them talking. I smell cigar smoke. No, wait, it's

SKELETON FOUND NEAR TRACKS

On May 31, 1905, the remains of an unknown soldier were discovered by three officers digging a trench about a hundred yards from Strachan Avenue.

The man's skeleton was located about two feet under the surface, and found with him were two old smoking pipes and a brass button. It is believed from the button that the man had been a soldier in the War of 1812.

sweeter … pipe smoke." She stopped near a doorway. "Oh, I don't like that room. I get the creepiest feeling from there."

"Is that cold storage?" Sheryl asked.

"It's just a horrible feeling, I am told to go in there, but I don't want to." They entered.

"It's a kitchen." Michele reeled back. "There's a shadow right there, it's a man. I don't like this feeling at all." She stopped and waved her hand across the back of her head. "Is there someone behind me? They just touched my hair!"

They moved on to the next room.

"There is a man in here by the name of John. He's in the corner. He has a big thick moustache and is wearing a hat," Michele told them, pointing. Sheryl took a photo. "Wow, as soon as your flash went off, I saw other people sitting here. There are three of them sitting in chairs right here. And he's standing over there." Sheryl and Michelle took pictures of the room.

"I get this feeling there is a hidden door somewhere, but I don't know where," Michele said.

They moved to another room. "Do we have a flashlight?" she asked.

The flashlights were in the kit bag at the other end of the hall. She headed off to get one, and as she neared the bag, she heard heavy footsteps coming up behind her. She stopped mid-stride and heard scuffling on the floor right behind her. She spun around but no one was there. She rushed back to the group, the flashlight now forgotten. "Did anyone come down the hall behind me?" she asked.

They all answered no.

Without the flashlight they moved on, stopping into a large room with a fireplace. "I don't like this room either, someone is ill in here. Oh, people slept in here," Michele said. "Hold on, I hear singing."

They pushed on down the hall.

"I'm really starting to get a heavy head down this end of the hallway," Michele said.

"Me too!" Sheryl added.

"There is a young male in here. He didn't live long. He was shot."

Everyone heard a male voice, and we all stopped.

Collection of the author

Michele investigating in the Barracks.

"Is that you? Give us a sign. We all heard you talk. Can you speak again?" Michele asked.

The voice recorder captured an EVP of a male voice saying "Help."

"Can you move something, make a noise?"

Water started to drip in the slop sink.

"Who are you, what is your name? I'm not getting it, you have to say it louder!" Michele demanded.

The voice recorder captured a male voice saying "Piper." Pipers have been around almost as long as music itself. They played an important role within the military, playing tunes that told the stories of victories. Pipers were used in parades and military rituals and were responsible for rallying the troops in battle.

"How did you die? You were sick! How old were you? Twenty-two. They called you Gopher. That was your nickname?" Michele inquired, digging into his past. "There is a Benny, and a Lisa. I'm hearing music again, he's gone."

"I heard the music as well," Sheryl added.

On the last visit, Sheryl had a particularly bad feeling in a small, triangular room at the end of the hall, so she ventured off to see if she could find out what was going on in that space. It felt different this time, not foreboding, and the sensation of being pushed away was no longer there.

While I was packing the equipment, Paul and Amanda explored the floor. Paul heard whispers but could not determine where they were coming from.

As Amanda stepped into the doorway of a theatre room, she saw a light move across the room towards the far wall. Just as the light seemed to arrive on the opposite side of the room, there was a loud thud and the light vanished.

The three of us headed down to the basement to meet up with the rest of the group.

Amanda stopped outside a large room near the women's washroom, where she had the distinct feeling of being watched. She looked in from the doorway; it was dark, with a little bit of light coming in from the windows high up on the walls. She saw a lot of movement in there — shadowy shapes of heads passing in front of the windows. She decided to take a picture before moving on. The photograph shows a lot of translucent circles in the air. Taking pictures from outside the room or in several other rooms did not produce these orbs.

It was time to go. We climbed the stairs and headed outside. Christina called security, and the building was secured and re-armed.

Paul needed a few days to analyze the surveillance footage, and we met later that week to see what he had found.

SURVEILLANCE RESULTS

From the basement camera, EVP caught two male voices, inaudibly. "Come here," then more whispering. The lights seemed to flash and there was a long pause. They started whispering again. "Come here."

"Henry."

The sound cut in and out.

The first floor camera caught a tapping sound and an EVP of an older male voice saying, "Wait, Jenny."

The camera captured me, Paul, and Amanda coming down the stairs and heading to the exit. There was an EVP of a male voice saying, "They are leaving."

From what sounded like some distance from the camera came an EVP of a young girl crying, "Daddy!"

The sounds of clanging tin came from various parts of the floor and different rooms. A male voice seemed to get angry. He was huffing and there were heavy banging sounds and heavy footsteps. An EVP male said "Come here!"

An EVP of a woman said "Jenny."

On the top floor camera, the sound of banging started immediately. Two males whispered, and the sound of a door opening could be heard. Behind the camera were a total of twenty light taps in succession, and then a sound of metal crashing on metal.

Then came a very odd sound. We can only describe it as the sound you would get when you bend metal, let it go, and it reverberates like a spring.

There was a lot of movement at the far end of the hall, subtle light changes and a very small dot of light that moved on a horizontal level. Along with the movements came random knocks and the sound of rustling fabric.

Although the images are dark and very hard to see, both our impressions were the same — it was a female holding a lit candle and trying to get someone's attention by knocking on the room doors.

Paul had made an important observation of something quite intriguing while analyzing the surveillance footage. He had noted that each time a team member passed the camera, the lights would appear to darken and then brighten, making them seem to flash or flicker. This was due to the auto lens iris: as someone passed the camera, their body would block out most of the light so the iris would open wider to allow more light to enter the lens, but once they fully passed the camera, the iris would be fully open, and all the available light would flood in. The iris would have to adjust for this by closing the aperture, producing an effect that made the lights seem to flicker. He noticed that on many occasions the flickering would occur when seemingly no one was around the camera. He felt that spirits could possibly be passing in view of the camera, and for some reason their energy was affecting the iris, even though the camera was not able to see them. This was a great observation, and we would have to look at the science behind it to see if we could somehow make improvements to how the camera viewed its environment.

Fifth Investigation

Stanley Barracks
February 2010

Paul, Sheryl, Alex, and Me

We met Linda and Christina at the General Services Building and drove out to Stanley Barracks, where security was waiting to open the door for us.

We entered and quickly went to work setting up the surveillance equipment. It is my group's priority to get the surveillance up and running as quickly as possible. We placed one camera in the basement at the furthest easterly point looking west.

As we worked, Sheryl looked at me then down the long hall. "It normally feels crowded, but tonight it seems empty," she said. I realized she was right — it did feel completely different to the other visits.

We moved upstairs and placed one camera facing east. Paul laid out a large plastic garbage bag at the end of the hall, where we had recorded activity on our last visit. He then laid out a thick coating of baby powder over the bag. It was his hope this evening to capture some physical sign in the powder.

Alex motioned to get our attention. We looked at him and he pointed to a twenty-five-pound fire extinguisher swaying slowly on its wall mount. No one was near it, so we checked the area and could not find anything that would cause it to move. Alex placed his hand on it and stopped it from moving then stepped back. It remained motionless.

Courtesy Exhibition Place Archives

Stanley Barracks

THE LOCK-UP

We proceeded up to the top floor, where we set up one camera looking east and another watching the west stairs, which is where we had previously recorded whispers.

With all cameras now recording, we began our tour of the building on the second floor. Checking and photographing each room, we made our way to the main floor, where a security officer joined us. After a few minutes of discussion,

Security personnel pride themselves on due diligence, so it becomes frustrating when a job well done is undermined in some way. This is what occurs at Stanley Barracks. Security on their patrols will secure the interior doors of the building only to find them unlocked and ajar upon their next tour. Where it becomes unnerving is when the alarm system verifies no one has entered the building since their last patrol.

we decided to split into two groups. Linda, Christina, and I went to the basement and picked a large room to sit in quietly and listen. Paul, Sheryl, Alex, and the security officer wandered the upper floors.

Linda used the parabolic microphone and stepped into the hall. She turned east and pointed the microphone dish towards the bathrooms, where she detected whispering.

The other group moved down the far west stairs and joined us in the basement. As they arrived, Paul paused to do a quick sweep of the area with the parabolic microphone and heard a child's giggle. The security officer walked back to him and asked if he had heard anything. Paul handed him the device, and the officer heard whispering coming from a mechanical area. Perplexed, he left the six of us in the basement and returned to his duties.

Everyone started commenting on the lack of activity we were detecting that night.

I've seen many haunted places do this from time to time without rhyme or reason. We have come to call it "GCE," or "Ghost Convention Elsewhere."

We continued to tour the building without incident, and to Paul's disappointment the powder was undisturbed. We cleaned up, packed the equipment, and made arrangements for our next visit.

SURVEILLANCE RESULTS

On the second floor, the image had returned from what we had recorded on our last visit, although it did not disturb the powder Paul had left on the floor.

There was a small light that seemed to move slowly from side to side at the end of the hall, and something large and black moved, blocking out the white walls. Both the light and this shadow seemed to move together. There was a series of bangs.

In the basement the camera recorded the sound of footsteps, a door opening, and a dog barking. The camera caught me walking down towards the camera to pack up. An EVP of a male voice was recorded in the bathroom area adjacent to the camera, saying "Let me be." It was an aged, raspy voice.

On the first floor the camera recorded a male EVP saying "Jenny." There was a high-pitched sound that went in and out, source unknown. Alex also recorded this sound on his hand-held digital recorder as he was touring the floor.

An EVP of a young girl called "Dad, Dad."

Paul and I had a long discussion of whether we should continue in the barracks or just move on to a new building. There seemed to be a sharp decline in evidence being recorded, and we could possibly have gathered everything available from the building. But intuitively we felt there was something more, something bigger, hiding just under the surface.

This is the conundrum faced by the investigator. The appearance of a lack of paranormal activity could suggest there is little or none to be found, but in our experience it could also mean there is something important being hidden, and the spirits that inhabit the dwelling stand quietly by hoping you will simply go away. We have also discovered that if we remain persistent and there is further information to be gained, they can't help themselves and will, as we say, give up the ghost. It is a love-hate relationship. While they love the fact that they can interact with people and get a positive response, on the other side of the coin they can hate you for being there as well. At best we will gain everything, at worst we waste a night's work.

We decided to go back, so I made the call to get permission.

Sixth Investigation

Stanley Barracks
March 2010

Paul, Jim, Darrin, Michele, Linda, Christina, and Me

The team arrived at the General Services Building, where we met Linda and Christina. They had arranged for security to meet us at the barracks, so we piled into our cars and drove over to the front of New Fort York. Security was waiting for us and opened the door. Darrin and Michele were running late, so we decided to set up the equipment so that when Michele arrived we could get straight to work. We placed one camera on the first floor looking into a large room. One camera was placed in the basement just outside the men's bathroom looking west down the hall.

Darrin and Michele arrived a few minutes later. Paul had his digital camera and recording system, Jim would handle the parabolic microphone, Darrin had brought his movie camera, Michele was wired with a digital recorder with external microphone, and I had my camera and an array of other equipment. We started at the west end of the second floor, where we would do a room-to-room investigation from top to bottom.

We arrived on the upper floor, and Michele led us into the first room. She stopped. "There is a heavy feeling in here. A man walks around in here, and he has a heavy breath. There is more than one, I hear them whispering."

Darrin called me over to where he was standing. "I hear them whispering, and when it's all quiet the sound meters on my camera are jumping."

I looked towards Jim. "Anything?" I asked.

He pointed the parabolic towards the back of the room. "Heavy breathing," he replied.

"Who?"

He shook his head. "None of us!"

"What direction?"

Jim pointed with the parabolic. "In the far corner."

Paul stepped in and took several photos.

"There are three in here," Michele said.

"Can you give us a sign that you are here?" I called out.

"I get the name Andrew. Are you here, Andrew?" Michele asked. "Andrew, can you give us a sign that you are here? You've let me hear your name, and I know you have two friends with you."

Pause.

"Humm, I hear 'maybe,'" Michele said.

"We don't mean you any harm. We have come a long way to find out who is here. Please give us a sign," I said.

"Something in here has wheels, I hear that sort of sound," Michele said.

We searched the darkened room and discovered a four-wheel dolly at the far end.

"I feel that it is moved around somehow," Michele said. She turned her attention back to the male spirit. "Andrew, can I call you Andy? Oh no, okay, Andrew. Andrew, can you give us a sign? Knock on something, move something?"

There came a slight knock from the far side of the room. We all heard it, and I looked to Jim for further confirmation. He was wide-eyed and nodding.

Michele thanked the spirit. "There is another one named Bill or Billy. I don't know if he is connected to the other ones in here. They come and go."

We stepped out on to a landing to the back stairs.

"I get disoriented here," Michele said.

"Me too, there is something with these stairs," I added.

We crossed the landing to the room across the hall.

"I'm hearing a child, running, giggling. Jenny, is that you?" Michele asked.

We all picked up a perfume scent.

"Jenny, is that you, honey?" Michele asked, looking towards the back of the room. "Okay, something is behind me, something just moved behind me. Jenny, if that is you, you are more than welcome to come and follow me around."

We stepped out onto the landing again.

"I don't like these stairs," Michele said as we started down.

"Are we staying on the second floor?" Paul asked.

"Yes, but we have to go down to get back up, as the stairs divide the floor," I explained.

Michele jumped back and almost knocked into me. "Whoah, there was a man standing right there, I don't know where he went now. He has dark, receding, slicked-back hair. Oh, the little girl is still with us, she looks tomboyish."

We moved on to the next room.

"They come and go in this room, no one stays in this room. Okay, standing in this room, I get a pain that shoots down my arm; my left arm now feels useless. Someone in here had a condition or injury," Michele explained.

After a long pause we moved on.

"Stepping into this room, I'm getting a very strong presence of a female. I'm seeing beds. One, two, three beds." Michele paused. "A child is dying, died there." She gestured to the corner of the room by the window. "He looks like he is maybe in his teens. They are putting cool cloths on his head. I get the letter D. This room is heavy; it feels to me like a sick room."

We moved on down the hall.

"There are more beds in here. There is a man sleeping here. He's snoring. He is a large man, balding, with hair on the sides. He has a uniform hanging beside his bed. I am picking up cigar smoke. Wait, I hear someone yelling Anna, Annie!"

We all smelled the perfume again and then it vanished.

"Jed, he passed from a heart attack, and a Marie, children connected to her, she moves the furniture around. As the sun comes in it is too hot for them," Michele explained.

"I'm picking up music," Jim stated.

"More like humming," Michele added.

We entered another room and Michele stopped abruptly. "How dare I enter this room unannounced? There is a person of high rank in here. Lieutenant David something. Hum, there was a fire down this end of the building."

Christina told us that she was examining some documents on the history of the fort and would get back to us about whether a fire did occur here.

Paul and I looked at each other. We both thought of the surveillance footage we had recorded on the two last visits. We stepped out into the hall to be away from the rest of the team.

"Could have been a fire," I said.

"And they are banging on doors to alert everyone else."

"Very possible."

We walked back down the long hall to the dreaded west stairs to move on to the first floor.

Michele paused. "Have you ever had a dream where you are being chased and you just couldn't run fast enough to get away from the person chasing you? That's the image I'm getting on these stairs. Someone fell down here."

As we arrived on the first floor, we discovered a possible source for the smell of perfume — boxes of hand soap, and lots of them. Although some of the team felt that what we smelled upstairs was more like perfumed powder, we had to err on the side of caution and discount the roving perfume smell.

Right after our discovery we all detected a fleeting cigar smoke smell. "It's a sweet smell," Michele added.

We moved on down the hall into the next room.

"Someone just cleared their throat, a very strong presence in here. Peter. He is not alone. A Scottish name, Macpherson, he has lots of medals, and only one leg. There is that cigar smoke again. Give us a sign you are here," Michele requested.

Something moved in the corner of the room, and we all heard it.

"I heard the name Kevin, very clearly," Michele reported.

We headed back out into the hall.

"A lot of kids come and go here, Cassy, Cassandra Lynn."

I could see Michele was getting tired, so we all agreed to take a much-needed break. Paul and Jim volunteered to pick up coffee and soft drinks, and Darrin went to the basement to use the washroom. Upon their return Paul asked where Darrin was, and Linda said he went downstairs but had been gone for a while. Paul went downstairs looking for him and found him listening in the washroom. Darrin reported that after he came down, he heard someone else walking down the hall and enter the bathroom, but no one else was there. The two returned to sit with the rest of the group on the first-floor landing.

I checked my watch, and it was time to switch the tapes on the basement system. I headed downstairs and walked to the end of the hall, ejected the tape, and replaced it with a new one. As I was walking away, the audio recorded a raspy male voice saying "Bastard" and a loud bang. I heard nothing at the time and kept walking to meet up with the group.

The team gathered the equipment and headed down into the basement. A sound was recorded on Michele's microphone that sounded like a scream. Later analysis would show that it was not a scream at all, but something more sinister — it was a growl. It made my blood turn cold. I'd had the unfortunate experience of hearing a similar growl many years before, coming from something with evil intentions, something that had never been physical. This meant two things: something very tragic had occurred here in the past which drew this entity to this place, and we unknowingly were about to walk directly into it.

As we descended into the basement, the surveillance camera at the far end of the hall recorded our movements. It also recorded a man's raspy voice screaming "Annie!" in anger, as if she were near us and he wanted her to come to him.

There was the sound of something hitting the camera, and the unit moved slightly.

Michele said, "There is a weird energy here." We entered a room. "There are women here setting up tables. They are wearing old-type dresses. I still feel there is a tunnel hidden here, somewhere."

The camera saw us thirty-five feet away, but no one heard the loud bang that the audio recorded.

We moved to the next room. "This room always freaks me out," Michele said as we arrived at the door. She stopped. "There is a shadow right in front of me, I can't tell if it's a man or woman. It's moving to the back of the room."

Everyone heard shuffling sounds crossing the room, but none of us were moving.

"Can you give us a sign you are still here?" Michele asked.

A voice recorded, but it was not speaking in English. It was possibly Ukrainian.

We entered the kitchen.

"Ally, Allison, Margaret, the two of you are here. Please give us a sign."

Several of us smelled baking bread.

Then we were distracted by the sound of metal on concrete from the next room. We moved to the great room and found it empty. As I entered the room, I tripped over a twisted piece of metal lying on the floor, and it spun across the tiles.

"That was the sound!" Paul said. I tapped it again with my foot, and the sound was unmistakable.

Courtesy Paul Palmisano

In this photo of the kitchen, Paul discovered an unknown mist in front of the windows.

"But who moved it the first time?" Darrin asked.

Michele stepped forward. "Something pushed me. I could hear them say 'Go, go' from behind me."

The room went cold, and everyone immediately noticed the drop in temperature.

"Do you want us to leave? Then give us a sign," Paul said.

Darrin's camera light started to flicker, and he called me over. "My battery pack was about one-fifth used when we came down here. Now it's almost completely depleted."

There were noises from the far end of the room, and the room got even colder.

"Something touched my hand," Michele called out.

The team stepped out into the hall. As Michele and I tapped on a wood wall panel, an EVP of a male voice was recorded saying, "He's not here."

Michele led us into the women's bathroom, and immediately all seven of us experienced pain in our abdomens. The pain started to increase, and we had to get out into the hall.

We regained our composure and reentered the bathroom. "I feel sick to my stomach. Someone was murdered, stabbed, another had a head wound," Michele spat out.

The pain increased, and we all fell out into the hallway again.

The camera recorded a male voice screaming "Annie!" There was a giant bang and a small ball of blackness about the size of a baseball appeared out of nowhere and went into the women's washroom.

"That is so strange how we all experienced the same thing," Michele said.

"Yeah. How much energy would it take to manifest that type of pain in seven people at the same time?" I asked.

"I felt severe pain on the right side of my head," Darrin added.

We were practically standing on the camera, and it still recorded crashes and bangs that none of us could hear.

We moved towards the men's bathroom, and Michele stopped at the doorway. "Horrible energy. He is very angry. He hurts people, a manipulator. He is moving behind me now. He takes advantage of women. He is the one who killed a woman in that bathroom. He abuses women, not his first. He also killed a man, and he himself was killed down here." There was very heavy breathing recorded on Michele's microphone very close to her that sounded like a man.

Christina's hands started to flail and she stepped forward, her eyes full of tears.

"What happened? Are you all right?" I asked her.

"I have to go!" she said and headed off in a rush for the stairs.

"He is hiding like a coward. Yeah. A coward who beats up women." Michele was disgusted and stepped back. "Not nice at all."

Paul turned the camera to face inside the washroom.

We fell back and regrouped; we needed to check on Christina.

The team met up on the first floor landing, where Linda and Christina were standing.

"What happened?" I asked.

"Something engulfed me, very cold, and the feeling of a deep sadness came over me. I kept hearing 'I don't want to be here, I don't want to be here,' over and over. Just panic!"

Michele stepped in closer. "She is clinging to you for help and safety. Humm ... a Daniela?"

"I just got goose bumps!" Christina reported. Michele did a cleansing to remove Daniela from Christina.

We took a break, and several of us went outside to get some air. Paul called out as a shadow of a person crossed the window in the basement men's bathroom. In the basement the camera recorded a growl, loud and hollow, a warning.

The team reassembled, and we headed back down to the basement. Christina and Linda decided to stay on the landing. As we passed through the doorway, Michele stopped. "I heard talking. Couldn't tell what was being said."

Paul stormed down to the men's bathroom. "Anyone here who wants to talk with us? I'm talking to the one who wants to be left alone. Can you give us a sign? Are you a man in uniform? What did you do to the woman down here? Did you kill her? Why do you want to be left alone? If you are a man in uniform, why don't you come out and talk with us? I think you are a coward, you hide in the shadows. Come on out and talk with us. If you are a man who wears a uniform, you don't deserve to wear it." Paul was pushing for a response.

Michele cried out in pain as she stood next to the cubbyhole. "My back, what's on my back!" she yelled out. Darrin and I moved in next to Michele, and as she pulled the back of her sweater up, her injury was immediately noticeable.

"Man, you've got two large scratches along the right side of the small of your back!" I told her. The area was very hot to the touch. "Maybe we should step out."

"No!" she said, standing her ground. We gave her a moment to recover, and she wanted to continue.

"I know the type, picks on women, and I bet he kicks little dogs too," I called out.

"I know you hurt that woman down here," Michele said. She paused a moment. "I heard him say 'I got her.' He's laughing."

She led us back to the women's washroom.

"We're in here now. Where is the coward? Tell us you want to be left alone," Paul yelled.

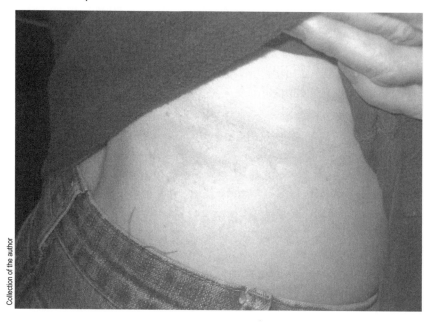

The scratches on Michele's back were clearly visible.

77

"These two keep playing through this event," Michele said.

"Are they trapped, or do they stay here because they like it here?" I asked while snapping pictures.

"He's here!" Michele reported.

"It's getting cold," Jim called out from the doorway.

"It really feels cold now," Darrin said.

"We asked you to come in, so come in," Paul called out.

"You are dirt," Michele started. "Daniela, can you come to me? Come to me." Michele stopped for a moment. "It's very draining. She will not come because he is here."

"Where is the coward?" Paul called out.

The camera recorded an EVP male voice, saying, "Catch me."

Michele again cried out in pain, throwing her hand to her back. "Scumbag!" This time she had another longer scratch under the first two. "Is it bleeding?" she asked.

I checked with my flashlight. "No. It's really red though."

"It burns. Jerk!"

"There are people talking in the hall," Paul reported.

"I'm stronger than you think. You don't scare us!" Michele told him. "Smug. He says 'I got you.'"

"Push me! You're a coward. Push me and we'll leave. Oh, 'cause I'm not a woman?" Paul asked. "Anything you want to add?" he asked me.

"No, I think you've covered it."

"I can't hear you, what do you want?" Paul asked.

"I hear a female, she is saying 'stop it, stop it,' over and over," Michele reported.

This was getting out of hand. We needed to reassess the haunting. We had an entity that had attacked twice, and we were pushing him hard. Who knew how far he might go? It was time to regroup and work out a plan for dealing with him. I advised the team of this and we began packing up the equipment. As we walked down the hall, Paul and I looked back towards the washroom. "We'll be back!"

SURVEILLANCE RESULTS

Four days later, Paul reviewed the surveillance. We met to go over the EVPs and to assess what happened Saturday night. The first thing he told me was the first tape made in the basement was completely destroyed. We speculated that the entity caused the distortion, and when I came down to change the tape, and he saw we were going to do it all over again, he called me "Bastard."

The first-floor camera that had been situated at the furthest easterly wall in the hallway faced into a large room with a smaller room in the far west end. Not long after the team moved off the floor, a male voice called "Annie." This voice was later identified as the voice in the men's bathroom. Each time he called her, there was a very loud bang near the camera.

The audio also recorded a sound like heavy furniture being moved in the room, but nothing moved on video.

Two small, unexplainable white lights came from nowhere and moved together towards the adjacent room at the back.

As we made our way down to the first floor, a male voice EVP was recorded saying "Keep quiet."

Another EVP of a male called "Jenny." Again there was a big bang near the camera.

The group moved down the hall towards the camera, and an EVP of a male was captured saying "Jenny, shhhh." It was followed by unintelligible whispering.

Then came a reply from the girl we assumed was Jenny. The EVP sounded like a voice of a young girl saying "Dad."

The sound of a large bell was heard, and the heavy gong sound reverberated for a few moments before a second gong was recorded.

The team proceeded to the basement, and there was the sound of someone running in the hallway.

A light appeared at the end of a long table at the far end of the room. It moved forward, stopped, then reversed direction, vanishing. There were walking, shuffling sounds and whispering that seemed to pass by the camera, followed by what sounded like a piece of metal bouncing across the floor, as if someone had thrown it towards the camera. There was a very long pause and then a sound like something very heavy being dragged down the hall. The very distinguishable scraping sound was followed by a pause, then it continued all the way down the hall. There was a sound like something steel banging against stone.

We returned briefly to the first floor, and a male voice called, "Jenny." Although we were standing there, we did not hear the sound of something being rolled down the hallway, the sound of wooden casters on the hardwood floor. As we started to leave, there was a crescendo of banging metal and tin from every direction.

The light appeared again on camera, and there was a big bang that seemed to send the light off into the adjacent room. All went quiet. An EVP of a male was recorded: "Get out of this place."

Paul saved the big discovery for last — a growl recorded on the basement camera.

The growl was a major concern. I knew that spirits who had committed heinous crimes had been found hiding in haunted locations for two major reasons: first, they feel they have skirted the issue of paying for their crimes by staying and hiding where they are, and second they feel a renewed power to exercise their will over their victim.

What complicates a situation like this is that places that have been witness to murder, suicide, and other tragedies have extremely negative energy. This negative energy will attract entities that were never physical, and in some circles can be referred to as demonic. They are by their very nature voyeuristic and will draw great satisfaction watching these souls intertwined in suffering. They may even trap these tormented souls in the place and add fuel to an already dreadful situation, for their personal amusement.

Walking into this type of unknown scenario could have truly dire consequences. The investigator poses a threat to this type of entity, and that threat comes in the way of assisting the victim to be free from the current situation and allowing them to break the entity's control. This would normally bring serious retaliation, and the growl was the first warning sign. I couldn't confirm if this was the case, but it had all the elements needed for such a scenario. If we were going to proceed, we would need a plan of action. Paul wanted to go back and ignore this male spirit, focusing on the female spirit to see if we could convince her to give us his name. After some discussion, we decided to move forward with this plan, understanding that it would more than likely anger this male spirit. I called Michele to tell her our plan and she agreed to join us. One rule was that we were not going to assist the spirits in leaving the building, and all agreed.

Meanwhile, I listened to the EVP of this spirit in the men's bathroom. "Catch me." This was a challenge I took personally. How I would do it was unknown at that point, but whoever he was, or had been, he was on my radar.

Seventh Investigation

Stanley Barracks with a Tour of the Horse Palace
March 2010

Paul, Sheryl, Michele, Peter, Grant,
Linda, Christina, and Me

Paul, Sheryl, Michele, and I arrived early and met Linda and Christina at the General Services Building to review some of the EVPs we had captured on our last investigation. They were astonished to hear this angry male spirit yelling for Annie as we all stood in the hall, obviously unaware of his activity.

After tonight's investigation of the Barracks, we moving on to a new location. We weren't abandoning the barracks, but we had a great deal of work to do elsewhere on the property, and with this level of activity, it could easily keep us busy for many months. I needed time to research the building's long history. We would be back.

Paul wanted to conduct a walkthrough of the next building to get a feel for the layout and determine the placement of our surveillance equipment. We drove to the Horse Palace, parking on the main floor next to a line of police vehicles. There had been reports of paranormal activity in this building from multiple sources.

HORSE PALACE TOUR

We began our tour on the main floor, walking the long rows of stalls. The whole time I was thinking that this was where many of the Canadian troops slept prior to being shipped overseas during the Second World War, my father being one of them as he trained here as a member of the Queen's Own Rifles.

We came to the main ramp that led up to the upper floor, an area that had seen some of the strange activity in the past. As we made our way up, Linda pointed out a restaurant that was also reported to be haunted. Michele and Sheryl were picking up subtle energies along the way.

Christina led us to a rear stairway, and we returned to the main floor. The team paused to look at some of names that soldiers had carved into the brick wall while stationed here in the 1940s. As we came to the bottom of the stairs, Michele heard a man laugh, but there was no one there.

The building was enormous and would pose a challenge for our surveillance equipment, but the team seemed excited to be there and felt there was definitely something worth investigating.

Linda contacted security and informed them that we were now heading over to Stanley Barracks. We drove the short distance to the New Fort, where we met up with Grant and Peter, who were waiting outside. After some quick introductions, we hauled the equipment into the building.

We had only requested the use of the east end of the building, since this was where most of the activity had been reported. The alarm systems remained armed on the west end, and I briefed the team on the access limitations.

As the rest of the team explored the rooms, Paul, Grant, and I set up two cameras in the basement on a cross pan configuration ten feet apart; this would give each camera the ability to watch the other, thus limiting the possibility of tampering. We did this specifically because whatever was down here liked to hit and touch the equipment. We set up the first camera at the base of the stairs looking towards the men's washroom.

Right away, the camera recorded audio that none of us heard at the time, that of a male voice, calling "Annie."

The second camera was set to record, and the three of us moved off to the stairs. As we entered the staircase, the same male voice yelled, "Get back from him!" then there was the sound of footsteps and movement around camera two.

Paul and I set up a third camera in a large room on the first floor, which resembles an old classroom. In the hallway just beyond the door, Paul laid out a green garbage bag then covered the surface with powder in hopes of capturing an impression.

We all retreated to an empty room on the second floor to drop off our backpacks and extra equipment. Some members of the team were on edge, since we didn't know what to expect. Everyone checked their equipment and changed batteries.

We decided to go directly to the basement, and I led the team downstairs. Michele, Christina, Sheryl, and I explored the kitchen while the rest of the team entered a room next door with a fireplace at one end. I walked to a swing door that joined the two rooms and looked through the small window in the door, accidentally startling Paul on the other side. He looked at me, shaking his head with a broad smile. "Don't do that!"

Michele looked up at us. "When you did that, I just heard a chuckle behind me." She paused, listening intently. "Someone just called to Annie."

Paul saw a flash of light from the back of the room. "Did anyone just take a picture?" he asked.

The camera outside the door recorded each of the team responding no to his question, with an EVP of the same male voice that had called Annie earlier, saying "Yeah."

The team moved across the hall to the women's washroom. As we entered, the lights in the hall seemed to dim.

"Annie, I know you are here. Can you come close to me, make a sound?"

"I feel off balance, my stomach feels sick. Annie, is that you giving us those feelings?" Michele asked.

There was a faint sound that everyone heard.

As Michele attempted to make contact, an EVP was recorded in the hallway of a male voice, saying "Oh yes, are they ..." with the sentence becoming unintelligible.

"'Step back!' I just heard her say." Michele stepped back. "It's very draining in this spot. She is warning us not to come back here."

Michele felt that the spirits were fleeting and either unable or unwilling to communicate. Everyone walked out into the hall towards the men's room.

As we entered, a male voice was recorded: "That bitch is right beside me!"

Paul moved to the centre of the room. "Where's my little buddy?" he asked.

The audio captures an EVP of a male voice saying "Right here."

"I feel like I'm being choked, like I can't breathe. I'm getting a *D* initial, but they come and go. I also get the name Thomas, but she doesn't fear him. 'Why don't you stop, why don't you stop,' I keep hearing over and over," Michele reported, placing her hand to her throat.

"Can you tell us his name, Annie, Daniela? Can you let us know you are here? Be strong, give us a sign. I just heard 'no.' It's so quiet now."

Michele couldn't open lines of communication, so we decided to take a break and head outside for some air.

As we started to head out of the washroom towards the stairs, Paul put his arm up as if placing it on the shoulder of an imaginary person standing beside him and mockingly said, "Let's go, Annie."

The EVP recorded a male voice near the washroom saying "Yeah."

As we left the floor, there came a loud bang near the camera, then an even louder bang from the far end of the hall. Near the camera a female voice said "Bob!"

A male responded, sounding angry. "Fuck you, damn it!" He then screamed, "Annie, Annie!"

All went quiet.

Paul and I returned to the basement and placed a large green garbage bag on the floor in the centre of the women's washroom, covering it with powder. We then left the floor.

A male EVP called "Annie." There was a crackling sound followed by a big bang.

Another male EVP said, "Come Dave ... come Dave."

I met up with Michele outside. "So, we seem to be getting a lot of warnings from this female. Are you sure you want to continue?" The team's safety was my primary concern.

"It's what we came for," Michele said. She led us back to the basement and straight into the women's washroom. As we arrived, Christina noticed she had water drops on her coat all around her waist. How they got there is unknown.

Peter stepped into the fireplace room, and the male voice was recorded yelling "Annie."

"I just heard steps behind us," Michele reported.

"So did I," Paul said, looking back into the hall.

Michele and Paul wanted to start a system of communication using knocks: one for yes and two for no. "Is this okay?" Michele asked.

"Yes," a male EVP replied. There was one knock.

A male EVP said, "Damn it Annie … Annie." A woman's voice replied, but the content was unknown. Then the sound of wood cracking was recorded. There were a lot of voices being recorded, but nothing could be interpreted.

Michele examined the powder. "Is that a small footprint and handprint in the powder?"

A female EVP replied "Yeah."

"Looks like the right foot and right hand," I added, examining the powder.

"They are small."

"Someone just pushed down on my shoulder. Whoever it was is gone now," Michele said. Her digital recorder picked up faint crying. "I've got a cold spot here," she said, extending her hand.

"It is colder here," Paul said, stepping in.

As Michele waved her hand through the cold area, she pulled it back. "Something just touched my hand. Annie, Daniela, are you here?" Michele laughed. "It's like a game of cat and mouse. Don't be shy. Let us know you are here."

Christina surprised the team. "I'm getting tiny jabs in my side. I hear a voice saying 'I don't know why I am here.' Do you have to stay here?"

Christina looked at Michele. They both simultaneously heard a "Yes."

"What's the gentleman's name? Is he a gentleman? I didn't think so either." Concern crossed Christina's face. "She is getting too close now."

"Someone is behind me. It's becoming cold again," Michele told us. "She's with him."

"There are two men!" Sheryl called out, sensing them.

Michele felt there was a male by the name of David. A male EVP yelled, "Dave, shut the hell up…!"

The stall door began to bang.

A male EVP said, "Annie. Ha ha. Annie … Annie get back … get back … here!"

"Someone is behind me. I feel fingers on my back, pulling my shirt," Paul told me while stepping into the bathroom.

Two knocks came from the hallway.

Something again touched Paul's back, and he immediately began to feel ill and agitated.

A male EVP said, "Huh, Annie come."

A female EVP was yelling, "Anne Marie!"

"Okay, can I provoke?" Michele requested.

"Go ahead," I said with a nod, concealing my concern.

"You like to pick on women. I really don't like you and I know you don't care. We don't want you here. We want you to leave. You don't belong here. Get out of here. Pack your bags and take a hike, fella!" Michele said loudly.

Sheryl and Michele all heard someone say "No."

"I just heard 'I beg to differ!'" Christina said.

"No, he doesn't want to go. He's not going anywhere," Michele said.

Paul stepped in. "Well, get used to us pal, 'cause we are coming back every day!"

Michele got poked in the shoulder. "Annie, Daniela, can you help me get rid of him?" She put her hand to her stomach. "Tough guy. Come on. Oh, he's doing the thing with the stomach again. I'm not afraid of you."

"Is that the best you've got?" Sheryl asked.

"The stomach thing's gone now," Michele said.

Then she cried out and almost fell to her knees. Peter and I stepped in close to her.

"I heard an impact. Are you all right?" Peter said.

"Crap, that hurt. Something hit me in the back!"

She lifted the back of her sweater and revealed a red mark that was quickly turning to a bruise. The mark resembled a boot heel.

"The bastard kicked me in the back! What a coward. He attacks women from behind … man, it burns … Is that all you got? That is nothing, buddy. I gave birth to five kids!" It took a moment for Michele to recover. "He likes to attack from behind, always from behind."

"He ran away like a coward." (Sheryl)

There was tapping all around the room.

"What was that?" (Paul)

"What did you hear?" (Peter)

"Tapping."

"There it goes." (Michele)

"Come on, a bit louder." (Peter)

"It's over here now. Annie, Daniela, is that you?" (Michele)

"Why don't you move upstairs?" (Paul)

"They can't." (Michele)

"Can you knock once for yes and twice for no?" (Paul)

"Can you give us his name?" (Michele)

Two knocks were heard.

"Can you give us the first initial of his name?" (Michele)

"I just had something touch my hip." (Sheryl)

"How many?" (Peter)

"Two." (Michele)

"That's a no." (Peter)

"They're gone … he's back. That's why they are gone," Michele told us.

"Do you know Jenny upstairs?" Paul asked. "Would you like to take a break with us? You could come upstairs with us so you don't have to be around him."

There were two knocks.

An EVP of a female child was recorded saying a long drawn out "no."

Everybody's stomach began to hurt again.

"Annie, Daniela, you know you are safe with us," Michele said.

There were two immediate knocks.

We headed upstairs for a break.

Several members of the team headed outside while Michele, Sheryl,

Linda, and Christina entered a sitting room on the first floor. As they entered, there was a rapid succession of bangs, almost like a drum roll. This incident was recorded on the main floor camera's audio system as well as Michele's digital recorder. When it was later analyzed, it sounded like someone running away, the sound trailing off in the distance. I theorized that this might have been the spirit girl Jenny.

While outside we noticed that the window on the first floor was open. The window was west of the main door, which meant no one on the team had access to that part of the building. Several of the team had photographed the face of the building when we arrived that evening, and we easily verified that this particular window had been closed earlier. I immediately reported this to Linda and Christina.

The team reassembled in the basement.

"I'm getting a creepy feeling on my left side, pressure," Sheryl told us.

"Oh, it's colder," Michele said.

"It feels like it's a male."

"Do you think it's him?"

"I don't know, but I'm getting a pain in my head right now."

The team moved away from the basement. Grant, Peter, and I investigated a small theatre on the first floor. Paul moved from room to room, and the rest of the team took up positions in the first-floor sitting room.

On a previous visit, the voice of a person speaking a foreign language was detected in the theatre. This evening there didn't seem to be anything out of the ordinary, so Grant joined the rest of the team and Peter and I met up with Paul. We headed into the basement to change the surveillance tapes. As we passed the fireplace room, we all heard a few keys played on a piano — there was no piano in the building.

In the first floor sitting room, Michele attempted an automatic writing session with Sheryl's assistance. Automatic writing is a technique used by psychic mediums to channel spirit energy. This energy apparently manipulates the medium to write messages conveyed by a spirit on paper. The medium will move into a trance state and start making circles on the paper with a pen. The pen will not stop moving until the session is completed.

Michele started to write as Sheryl kept a supply of fresh paper under the pen.

Stewart got hurt
Murder
Murder
Murder
Daniela is here
Murdered by David
He is here won't let us leave
Sarah is here too
M
Wants to go
But
They won't let us leave

Sheryl asked, "How many are here?"

There are seven of us here

The session ended and Michele took a few moments to recover, since it was obviously mentally and emotionally draining for her.

"Do you want to rest?" Sheryl asked.

"No, let's keep up the momentum," Michele said, getting up.

The team headed directly to the women's washroom in the basement.

"Daniela, Annie, who is David?" Michele asked.

Peter's digital recorder captured a deep, hollow sound like a heartbeat, and Christina reacted to the question by taking a deep breath.

"Who is Stewart? Are they here? Can you knock one for yes, two for no?"

Two knocks were heard.

"Is there a David here?"

There came a single knock, which all present heard.

"Is there a Sarah here? Can you write the initial in the powder? Could you do that?"

There was a low crying sound.

"Is that Annie?"

"Daniela." Christina felt that it was the girl.

"I heard it too," Michele said, looking at Christina. "Is Sarah your mother?"

"Did you hear a girl?" Paul asked.

"I heard that too," Michele replied.

"Okay, all the guys step out and just leave the girls in the washroom," I said. I wanted the men to move into the hallway to see if communication improved with the female spirits when they were less intimidated by a male presence.

"Is it better with just us girls?" Michele asked.

Two knocks followed.

"Did Stewart hurt you?" Two knocks.

"Did David?" One knock.

Something touched Christina's back, and everyone was on edge again.

"Do something with the powder," Michele asked.

There was movement behind her.

The men re-entered the washroom.

"Let's check the powder," Michele said. Several of us shone our flashlights down over the powder.

"There is a letter *D* in the powder," Michele observed.

"It's getting cold in here," Paul said.

I could sense the tension in the team, and I called a break. As the team climbed the stairs everyone heard singing from the first floor. We investigated and found nothing.

After some much-needed coffee, everyone headed back to the basement.

"I want to see that powder again," Michele said. "See the *D* ... Oh, there is a line through it! That wasn't there before. Now it looks like a *B*."

"It looks like someone took three fingers and stroked it through the letter," Christina said. "I just got a nursery rhyme in my head."

"Which one?" Michele asked.

"Mary, Mary quite contrary, how does your garden grow. Now I have major chills."

"Is there a Mary here?" Michele asked.

We all heard a big bang from upstairs, which was recorded on the surveillance system on the first floor.

"Let's try the automatic writing in here," Michele said.

Sheryl pulled up a chair from the corner of the room. Michele sat and tried to relax, and Sheryl handed her a pen and prepared the paper.

Linda's cell phone rang, and she excused herself to the hallway. As she moved past camera two, the EVP of a male voice was recorded, saying, "Oh, you're hot."

Back in the bathroom Peter said, "I'm hearing rapid knocks, maybe they are anxious to get started."

Michele was relaxed and prepared to begin when the pen flew out of her hand. "Oh, somebody doesn't want to talk to us."

We began again. It started off with flowing scribbles, but then the scribbles started to turn into words.

Hello again
I really like you
Being here with us
Help
He's here

Sheryl asked "Who?"

Stewart here
Here's mad

"I just got major chills," Sheryl reported.

Get out yes get out
David is here

Sheryl asked, "What is your name?"

I will never tell you
Sarah

He murdered us here
Help
Help
Someone coming Annie
My daughter

Sheryl asked, "Can you tell us what year it is?"

1
9
5
3

Sheryl asked, "Why are you upset?"

Baby
Baby dead
Help
Help
Help my baby
Killed
Her

Sheryl asked, "Who killed her?"

David
Help my baby
He's here
David here
Killed
Can you see her on the floor
David is a murderer

Sheryl asked, "What is your baby's name?"

Daniela
David killed my baby

Sheryl asked, "Was David her father?"

Angry scribbles tearing up the paper.
Get out get out
His blood is on the ...
He's here and won't let us leave
Worker
Can you feel her presence on the floor

The session ended, and I could see Christina was visibly upset. Tears were running down Michele's face. "That poor woman...."

The team was drained, and I couldn't tell how much more Michele would be able to take, so we called it a night. It was time to let this place rest — at least for a little while. I needed to take this information and see if we could find anything in the building's history that would corroborate our story.

While we were all in the basement, the surveillance system on the main floor was recording activity. A male EVP said "Jenny, you there?" A cat meowed throughout the recordings. It was interesting that on our first visit, I had captured a photo of a phantom tabby.

There were hollow bangs and the click of a door latch behind the camera. Something passed the camera, casting a large, black shadow on the fridge in the classroom. An EVP of an unknown woman yelled for Amanda. A strange light appeared on papers on one of the tables, and the sound of rustling paper was recorded. The toy Michele had left on the table drew the strange light to it.

It was disturbing to listen to the EVPs later. They indicated that these spirits where not only aware of us but were amongst us most of the night, directly commenting on our conversations and actions.

As we prepared to leave for the night, we saw a light go out in the room with the open window. Grant retrieved a spotlight from his van, and we went up to the window to look in. The light we discovered had not gone off, nor had it vanished. It seemed that the door to the office had been open, and the light we saw had been from the hall. The light had seemed to vanish when the door closed ... but who had closed the door?

As we were investigating, my car headlights started to flash, and the left blinker started by itself. As I walked back to the car, they stopped.

Paul was feeling extremely sick and left without saying goodnight. I checked on him the next day, and he was feeling better.

We couldn't understand the significance of the nursery rhyme, which referred to Mary Tudor (1516 to 1558), the daughter of King Henry VIII, who was also known as Bloody Mary. Queen Mary was a Catholic, and the growing of the garden referred to the 284 people she had put to death for following the Protestant faith.

After we reviewed the information and EVPs, I was starting to get a clearer picture of what might have happened in the basement, but I still needed verification. I now had this person's first name, given to us by Annie on EVP — Bob — and the first letter of his last name — *M*. He seemed to be in collaboration with this other male spirit, David. Although David was pointed out as a killer, I had a gut feeling that Bob was worse.

Eighth Investigation

Horse Palace
April 2010

Paul, Sheryl, Michele, Darrin, Jarred, Peter, Linda, Christina, and Me

The only time the Canadian National Exhibition has ever closed its gates to the public was during the Second World War. The Horse Palace was used by the army, the air force took over the Coliseum, which was temporarily renamed Manning Depot, the navy moved into the Automotive Building, and the Canadian Woman's Army Corps was stationed within Stanley Barracks.

The Horse Palace is a three floor Art Deco-style equestrian facility built in 1931; there have been multiple reports of haunting activity in the building. It is now the home of the Metro Toronto Police Mounted Unit. One officer stated that on many nights when no one was on the second floor, he would hear footsteps and horses moving around, but the floor would be devoid of people and animals.

PHANTOM HORSES

The stables on the upper floor of the Horse Palace are generally vacant. The staff of the riding academy located on the lower floor reported hearing horses moving around above their heads. One staff member brought their dog to the stables and was playing fetch. They tossed the bright red ball up the ramp to the upper floor, where the dutiful dog ran up after it. The dog returned to its owner without the ball, but a few moments later the ball bounced back down the ramp. There was no one on the upper floor.

Courtesy Exhibition Place Archives

The Horse Palace, 1931

Very few people know that there is a third floor. Considered to be more of a mezzanine, it is used for storage and roof access.

That night we had special permission to enter the second floor restaurant. This is where we would set up our surveillance equipment and our base of operations.

Linda opened the door with a long squeak of hinges, and the team entered. The setup resembled a western saloon with a long plank bar made of pine and oak barrels. Hanging on the walls was riding memorabilia such as hats, riding crops, and ribbons. Paul and I quickly went to work setting up our equipment. We placed a surveillance unit near the entranceway facing into the restaurant and covering the bar area. We placed a second system at the far end near the kitchen, looking back across the expanse of the dining floor towards the front door and a large fireplace. The team explored the various rooms and adjacent hallway, which serviced the washrooms and storage rooms.

Everyone conducted their equipment checks, and we headed out to explore the Horse Palace. As we exited the main door of the restaurant, Linda slid the heavy wood door closed, sealing the entryway and our equipment inside.

As we made our way between rows and rows of horse stalls, Michele and Sheryl picked up on subtle energies and cold spots as we pushed forward. Darrin and Jarred hauled their movie camera and boom microphone.

Christina, Linda, and I broke off from the rest of the team and they showed me the upper mezzanine level. As we entered, the energy was strange and disorienting. I felt dizzy. The floor there is large, with enclosed locked sections of wire mesh fencing. There is a rooftop access door, where we stepped out into the fresh air and took in a commanding view of the Exhibition Place grounds. There were rows of solar panels taking in the last rays of the day's sun. We moved back inside and walked to the stairway door. As we did, I felt not so much a push, but rather an energy helping me along, as if hurrying me out. I stopped and walked back. I turned and moved towards the door, and again I had the same sensation. I looked at Christina and told her about what I had just experienced, and she tried walking in the same area, with similar results. "Someone doesn't want us here. We'll have to bring the team up here," I said as we descended the stairs to the second floor.

We met up with the others as they were finishing their tour. Peter had been walking with his digital recorder activated, and as he walked amongst the many rows of empty stalls, he captured what sounded like a child's voice.

We arrived at the restaurant and set up two tables to sit around while we took a coffee break.

As we were sitting at the tables, we heard footsteps, the sound of women's high heels, just behind a divider wall that separates the washrooms and utility rooms from the bar. Several of us went to investigate. We checked the rooms and found nothing. After a few minutes of searching, we returned to the tables.

"We know you are here. Can you give us another sign?" Michele asked.

Several of us heard "Yes."

Banging came from the washroom area, and again we hurried over, but there was no one. Paul stepped into the washroom and looked around. He pulled paper towels from a wall-mounted dispenser, and each time the dispenser rotated, it made the same banging sound that we had heard earlier.

Michele saw a light from an adjacent room. Upon investigation we noticed that the windows to the attached room had been boarded up. The place where she had noticed the light changing was a hole in the wood, and it seemed as if someone or something had looked through that hole, momentarily blocking out the light. We examined the adjacent room, which was locked, and found nothing out of the ordinary.

This was turning out to be a game of cat and mouse.

As we finished our break, the team started to wander around in the restaurant, bar, and adjacent rooms. At the very back of the bar area was another divider wall to the kitchen. Sticking out of the wall was an old soda machine with a three-inch gap all around its edges. As Paul neared the divider wall, he noticed a pair of legs passing one of these gaps. He called to me because I was standing near the doorway to this kitchen area. "Where's Michele? Is anyone back there?"

I looked around the doorway into the space. "No one is in here. Why?"

Paul pushed past me into the room to see for himself. "I just saw two legs, as if someone walked past the back of the soda machine."

"What did they look like?"

"Legs, blue jeans. That's why I thought it was Michele back here."

Michele led the rest of the team to where Paul and I were standing, and Paul explained what he'd seen.

"We know you are here. Some of us have seen you. We have all heard you. We know there are at least two of you here. Can you give us a sign?" Michele asked.

"Bang on something, one knock for yes, two knocks for no," Paul added.

"I just heard 'I don't have to,'" Michele told us. "This spot is getting really cold."

The area behind her was cold compared to the rest of the room. We checked for open windows or air vents, anything that could create a breeze or explain the air temperature change, but found nothing. Within moments the cold spot was gone and the area was warm again.

We tried to open the lines of communication, but it had grown quiet.

I knew from an article in the daily paper on November 7, 1945, that during the war years there was an emergency medical station located in the Horse Palace. A streetcar had flipped over and injured twenty passengers at the Fleet Street loop, and the more seriously hurt were brought to the aid station at the Horse Palace. We searched the building for the most appropriate location, since we thought there might be spirit activity. The only area we could find that fit the requirements was the one currently used by the Metro Toronto Police Mounted Unit.

As we scoured the second floor, Christina and I stopped to look at a large area used as a shower for the horses. As we were talking, Christina saw the lights come on briefly at the food building. They flickered on for two seconds, then off again. "There is no one over there. That is so weird," she said.

"Maybe we need to have a look over there some time."

So I gathered the team, and Linda led us up to the mezzanine. On the way up the stairs I could hear the comments ahead of me filtering down. "This is weird energy up here," Michele said.

"I feel dizzy," Darrin reported.

"I've got a sick feeling, hard to breathe," Paul said.

"It's disorienting up here," Sheryl added.

Paul saw some movement in the back of one of the fenced-off areas and called to get my attention. We stood watching for a few moments. Suddenly, something banged in another section as if someone had tripped over a piece of metal and had sent it rattling across the floor.

"There, a light moved," Paul said, pointing excitedly to the spot.

"I saw it too."

We examined the floor, but there was no hole that light could have come through, so we stood, waited, and watched.

"I'm getting pain and sadness. There are multiples up here," Michele advised us.

Sheryl picked up the energy of a male near the roof access door. She sensed that he lived there and brought Michele over to show her the space.

"Oh, there is a male here," Michele told us.

"Depression," Sheryl added, and Christina agreed.

"Mike ... Mike. Is that your name?"

Jarred stepped in close with the HD movie camera and filmed Michele and Sheryl.

"It's Mike." Michele looked at Sheryl. "Give me your hands and see if we can give him enough energy to communicate with us. Why are you here? Why do you still roam here after your death? Wow, okay he didn't know he was dead," Michele added, shocked.

They took a moment.

Sheryl could sense the energy directly behind her, standing close to her.

"Touch Sheryl. He likes you," Michele said.

"It's getting cold around me. I feel him getting close," Sheryl said, smiling.

"He says he likes your hat. Why are you sad? Mike, why are you sad?"

Something unseen hit the boom microphone, and Jarred backed up.

"I think he put his arms around me," Sheryl said.

"It's very cold now. Remember, Mike, you cannot leave here to go with her. You cannot go with her. He's gone."

Just as she said that, Jarred jumped back.

"What happened?" Darin asked.

"Just as she said he was gone, there was, like, a shimmering heat wave that came from in front of them and came straight towards me."

Darrin later discovered that each time Michele had asked a question, the lens blurred. It was very quick, and he had a hard time explaining it, but a frame-by-frame analysis showed that the blur lasted exactly six frames of film each time. Looking closely at each frame, the blur does not encompass the entire frame but rather moves across Sheryl first, then over both Sheryl and Michele, then off Sheryl and completely onto Michele, continuing across each frame left to right until vanishing altogether.

"Did you get anything on him? An era?" Christina asked.

"Forties. He is more of a gentleman: moustache, hat, a dress shirt, but grubby. He really liked you, though," Michele explained.

Christina heard a faint "wooooo."

Someone suggested a break, and we headed outside to get some fresh air.

After our break, Linda led us back to the restaurant. When we slid the outer door open and entered through the creaky swing doors, we noticed that all our bags had been thrown off the table and now lay scattered across the floor. Everyone split up to investigate the area, checking the various rooms and snapping photographs at random. Paul aimed his camera at a large mirror above the front fireplace, then turned and looked at me. "Someone just hit my shoulder." This brought a flurry of camera flashes from every direction.

Michele headed over to the washroom, and as she reached for the swing doors, they slammed shut by themselves. She jumped back. She could clearly see through the windows in the doors. No one was on the other side. She paused a moment and then proceeded to the washroom.

When she returned, she told me what had happened. "Let's do a room by room check with Michele," I said. I gathered up the group and led them into the service hall. The team entered the women's washroom first.

Michele tried to open communication, asking if anyone was there. "We have heard you. Please come closer and speak with us or give us a clear sign that you are here."

There were sounds like whimpers that were barely audible. Something touched Christina and there was a low "umm" sound.

"Would you feel more comfortable if the men left? Then do that again, and they will leave." Christina felt a pinch on her baby finger and asked, "Was that you? Can you do that again?" This time Michele felt the pinch on her baby finger.

As promised, the men stepped out into the hall, leaving Michele, Linda, Sheryl, and Christina.

"Okay, they're gone. Can you communicate with us?" Right away Christina and Sheryl both got a sharp pain on the side of their heads. "Is that you doing that? Are there others with you?"

They heard mumbles, and everything went quiet. The energy started to change and everyone had an uneasy, creepy feeling.

The women came out into the hall and joined the men, who had been investigating the storage rooms. One of the rooms had an old chain lock on the inside, as if someone had stayed in there at one time.

We heard the paper roller in the men's washroom. We rushed into the room and found nothing. We piled out into the service hall and walked back to the swing doors. As we filed along the hallway, Jarred stopped dead in his tracks, and Darrin, who was directly behind him, backed away.

"Someone's pulling on my hood!" Jarred called out. Darrin watched as the hood on Jarred's jacket was tugged away from his back.

It was becoming a little unnerving, since whatever was here was starting to interact with all present.

As we arrived at the swing doors, Paul saw a shape outside the restaurant at the far end of the second floor. At first everyone thought it looked like a person standing there, but it was an optical illusion — it was just the way the shadow fell across the downpipe that ran along the corner of the wall. But as everyone was looking at this, I was watching a black shadow about eight feet to the left, which looked like a dog the size of a Labrador retriever. It moved around a hay cart then vanished. Paul and I walked to the location but found nothing. We returned to the restaurant and joined the others.

Although we were surrounded by roving cold spots and odd noises, it was late and our time there was drawing to an end. We collected our equipment and left the restaurant, locking the massive door behind us. We filed down the steep wooden ramp to the main floor and began loading the cars. Paul looked back towards the ramp and saw a black shadowy figure walking down to the bottom. It stopped and peered over the side at us then vanished. Paul checked the ramp, and what he had seen was nowhere to be found. What he did find was a handprint in the dust where it appeared as if someone had stopped and leaned over the side to

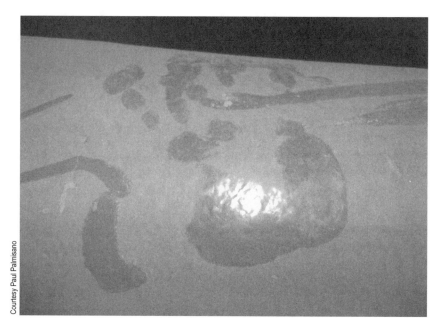

Courtesy Paul Palmisano

This handprint was left in the dust by whatever Paul had seen spying on us.

see where we were. It was very exciting that whatever it was had left its mark in the form of physical evidence.

Days later, Paul called with some disappointing news — the surveillance recordings from the camera at the back of the restaurant were nothing but static, and completely useless. The camera near the front door was a different story; it had functioned very well for the first thirty minutes, up to the point where we had left the restaurant for our tour. It had captured Linda closing the heavy sliding door and our voices fading off into the distance. All was quiet until there was a creak of the inner swing door and an EVP of a man saying something indecipherable. Then the machine inexplicably shut off. With all of our data lost, and with so much activity observed, I told Paul that the Horse Palace definitely warranted a second investigation. He immediately agreed.

Losing the data was the bad news — the good news was that Peter told me he had captured a very strange and important EVP from the second floor in amongst the horse stalls. It was a male saying, "You don't see me, I'm right here."

This was interesting in so many ways. It would appear that this spirit could easily perceive us, seemed to know he was dead and invisible, and had the ability to interact. We most certainly had to go back.

Ninth Investigation

Horse Palace
May 2010

Paul, Sheryl, Michele, Amanda, and Me

I had made arrangements for access to the Horse Palace, but unfortunately Linda and Christina would not be able to attend this time. I stopped at the General Services Building and spoke with security. As usual, they were very professional and accommodating.

When we arrived, Paul, Amanda, and I began setting up the equipment. This time I brought an extra surveillance system, allowing us three for the restaurant area. We placed two in the same locations as last time, and the third was placed facing the service hallway to the washrooms.

I decided to try an experiment and placed synchronized clocks in the foreground of each camera. Although all of our analysis equipment had counters, I wanted to see if there would be any noticeable time variation between areas; it would also act as a fairly good time stamp for our chronology of events.

Amanda walked away and took a seat in the middle of the room. She reported that when she entered the restaurant, she began to feel lightheaded and dizzy and was experiencing random waves of hot and cold. While sitting there, she felt two taps on her right

THE OFFICER AND HIS HORSE

An employee was cleaning inside the Horse Palace late one night during the Royal Agricultural Winter Fair when he saw a uniformed police officer walking his horse. The cleaner said hello as they passed. When the employee turned to look again, the officer and horse had vanished.

arm, then two taps on her left arm, and a moment later she felt a pinch on her right arm. My first impression was that this is exactly what nurses do when they take blood: the two taps are to look for a good vein, compare the right to the left, and then the pinch of the needle. Of course, this was just pure speculation.

At some point, Sheryl started to feel slightly dizzy as well, and Michele confirmed she was feeling it too. This phenomenon only seemed to be affecting the females, although Paul and I were sensing the waves of cold. Sheryl had to take a moment, as she began to experience a sharp pain in her left ear.

Michele saw a man dressed all in black and immediately felt a severe pain in her left leg. The figure vanished but left her with the impression that he had a wooden or prosthetic leg and that his name could be Roy.

The equipment was recording, and the five of us headed out into the Horse Palace to tour the second floor and mezzanine level. As we walked along the outer hall towards the horse stalls, we had the distinct feeling that we were being followed. As we rounded a corner, the team came to a halt — a black shadow started to turn the corner, startling us, then quickly retreated. I thought I saw it go into a nearby stall, and Paul and Michele thought it went back down the hallway. Wherever it went, it was nowhere to be found.

We continued on and climbed the stairs to the upper level. Sheryl and Michele entered first. "Mike, are you here?" Michele called out.

As I stepped in and walked to the middle of the hallway, I felt a strange, almost foreboding sense of unease. Something up there wasn't right, and felt it completely different from our last visit. Michele said she sensed extreme sadness. The group moved down towards the roof access door where we had encountered Mike last time.

I asked Amanda to walk down the hall, and as she came to an area that opened into a larger hall, she stopped dead. She looked at me and said, "I don't think so!"

"What's wrong?" I asked.

"I felt a hot breeze in my face and, like, a head rush."

After several attempts to open communications, we decided to come back later to try again. We went downstairs and headed outside for some air.

After a look around the exterior, the five of us returned to the restaurant. Paul called me. He had noticed that all the clocks we had set up were now on the floor. I checked the equipment and everything was still recording. As Paul and I reset the clocks, Amanda saw a tall, thin beam of light behind the bar that moved quickly towards the doors and vanished. She walked to the camera next to the swing doors and looked at the monitor; although we were not far away, she was now alone. As she started to walk towards the back of the restaurant, she heard the swing doors creak open slightly, as if someone was coming in. She looked back but no one was there.

After inspecting the rooms, the team converged in the centre of the restaurant area and sat around one of the tables. We were discussing some of the strange experiences we'd had when the sound of a door came from the bathroom area. Paul and I went to investigate but found nothing.

Amanda and I volunteered to go and get coffee for everyone. Paul had to come down with us to operate the door, leaving Michele and Sheryl in the restaurant. As they sat there talking, Sheryl's chair started to tremble then moved as if there was an earthquake. She leapt from the chair, terrified, her heart racing. Michele, who was sitting next to her, felt nothing.

After we returned, Michele got up and walked to the kitchen area. "I heard something move here." The rest of us joined her. She stopped and grabbed the wall to steady herself. "Something just walked through me."

"I just heard a woman's voice say 'no,'" Paul reported.

We waited, but all had gone quiet. I suggested we head back to the mezzanine level.

Michele suggested we all join hands. Michele, Amanda, and Sheryl gathered near the roof door and Paul scouted out the floor, but I just stood there with this nagging feeling that something was very wrong up here.

As they stood there holding hands, they tried to open communications.

Paul walked past me and I looked at him. "I have a bad feeling up here," I told him. He nodded but kept walking.

As the women tried to communicate, Amanda started to feel warmer, her eyes started to sting, and she felt as if there was someone beside her.

They all started feeling their hair being tugged, and Amanda felt a slight touch on her right cheek. She sensed a Bryan. Michele called out "Ben."

They stopped and looked around the room. "Mike is not here," Michele said.

I started to get a taste of blood in my mouth. "No, he isn't. He is afraid to be here right now. We should go."

As the team headed for the door, Paul set an audio recording system on the floor. Amanda said she had a bad feeling as well and moved to the door, almost bumping into Michele.

We headed downstairs and I led the team outside. I had no explanation for what I had experienced on the upper floor, but I hadn't survived this long by ignoring my gut feelings.

It was late, so we headed back to the restaurant and started packing up. We hauled the equipment to the ramp, and Paul and I had to go back and retrieve his audio system from the mezzanine and lock the door. Sheryl, Michele, and Amanda brought the equipment to the car and secured the restaurant while Paul and I climbed the stairs. Paul was feeling the same uneasiness as we neared the door to the upper floor. We entered with caution but, although the machine was all of ten feet from the door, it seemed to be a hundred yards away. Paul grabbed it and we hurried out, locking the door behind us.

SURVEILLANCE RESULTS

It was four days later when Paul called me regarding the surveillance recordings.

He reported that we had recorded some exceptional EVPs on our visit, but due to the size of the area, a lot of what was said had been lost.

We started with the camera that looked down the hall by the washrooms. There were a great deal of unexplainable sounds — banging and a whistle. At one point Michele and Sheryl were outside the washroom.

"Did that sound come from in there?" Michele asked.

"Yes," Sheryl replied.

An unknown male voice is heard saying, "Yeah."

As we were all sitting around the table talking, the camera from the rear of the restaurant recorded an EVP of a male voice, saying "Lower your voices."

There were whimpering sounds from a female voice, and a male voice said something inaudible.

Just before Sheryl jumped from her chair in panic, there was a noise like a very high-pitched whistle. We were not sure if the sound had anything to do with the chair moving.

On the camera at the front of restaurant, a sound like snapping fingers was heard. An unknown female voice called "yoo-hoo." An EVP of a male voice called out "Ed ... Ed."

Michele and Sheryl come through the swing doors on their way back from the bathroom and there was an EVP of a male voice saying "Thank you, cat witch bitch."

The cross pan cameras both recorded that that the clock at the front of the restaurant fell first, with the rear clock falling less than a second later.

As we were investigating the bar area, Michele moved along the bar and said "Give me a drink, I could die of thirst here."

She got a reply by EVP from a man: "Hang me."

It seemed that whoever this male voice belonged to, he was a character. He had a warped sense of humour and a serious attitude and seemed to be very smart, almost as if he had dealt with paranormal investigators before.

Paul held the last EVP back. He looked at me. "You're not going to believe this one. It's from the upper floor."

"Okay, let's hear it."

"This is when we go back up to retrieve the machine, it's right at the end."

I listened to the static. I heard us enter, then heard a gruff voice of a male saying "Get out! Get the fuck out!" The machine shut off.

"I heard that, and it gave me the creeps right away."

I just nodded.

Tenth Investigation

Press Building
May 2010

Paul, Sheryl, Michele, Linda, and Me

We picked up Linda and headed over to the Press Building. It is a remarkable structure designed by G.W. Gouinlock in the Beaux-Arts style. It was opened in 1905 and was home to the Canadian National Exhibition administration. It is the oldest original existing building specifically built for the CNE. What makes this building exceptional is the beautiful architectural design and the hi-tech heating and cooling system, which has been recently added. There are twelve thermal exchangers that extend 480 feet and use the Earth's natural geothermal properties to heat and cool the building. This allows this building to use minimal electricity while doing away with fossil fuel use altogether.

After security opened the door for us, we had a quick tour of the main floor. The women familiarized themselves with the building, and Paul and I headed upstairs to find suitable locations for our cameras.

As Linda, Michele, and Sheryl were talking in the hallway downstairs, Michele suddenly looked over her shoulder and said, "Oh, sorry." Everyone looked, but there was no one there. She told them she could have sworn I had come down and was standing behind her. She said a man dressed in black had been right there.

Michele was now picking up the name "Fred." They started to look around and noticed that many photos of past presidents of Exhibition Place were hanging in nice neat rows at the bottom of the stairs. They started searching for a photo with a man named Fred. Sheryl quickly

Courtesy Exhibition Place Archives

The Press Building, 1948

found one and pointed it out to Michele, but it wasn't the man she'd seen. They continued to search, and above the doorway to the stairs was another photo of a man named Fred who'd presided during the 1950s. Michele studied the photo for a moment and said, "That's the man I saw!"

Paul and I set up one camera at the top of the stairs and another in a long hallway that crosses the floor towards the washrooms. As we were setting it up, the hall light kept coming on then going off. Behind the camera was a lunchroom with coolers that were running, so we closed the door to reduce the sound. Paul wandered off to investigate the light. I set the system to record, and he called me over.

"This thing is on a motion detector," he said, pointing to the light switch. I looked at it and realized that from its location there would have been no possible way for us to have tripped it. But if we hadn't activated it, who had? We both started moving further away from the motion detector, trying to determine its range. Our position near the lunchroom was much too far away to activate the lights.

Paul and I started back downstairs to join the others, and we found them near the bottom landing talking about what had just happened. They showed us the photo of Fred.

Paul suggested that we head upstairs and let Michele lead to see if she could pick up on anything. At the top of the stairway, the first hall to the left leads to the washrooms and the lunchroom. To the right are offices and a ladder to the roof. Deeper into the floor is an open area and another hall leading to offices. The team climbed the stairs, and we all started exploring the various offices. Down the hallway to the left was a small office with no windows, and as we entered, both Michele and Sheryl described a horrible feeling of sickness. Michele decided to investigate that room later in the evening.

We continued our investigation, going room by room. As Michele led us into another office, Sheryl immediately felt a rush of dizziness. Michele looked around and said, "I don't like it." Linda mentioned to us that on occasion she was called to work in that office and never liked spending any time in there at all. Michele sensed a male presence in the room.

We continued going through all the other offices, and we took a quick tour of the "Queen's Bathroom," located on the second floor. Apparently, for Queen Elizabeth II's visit, the Canadian National Exhibition had built her a private washroom. The team then headed downstairs, and Linda continued showing us the offices on the main floor.

As we entered a room on the first floor, Michele felt ill and Sheryl got very dizzy. The strange thing was that the room was directly beneath the small office upstairs that they had felt uncomfortable in.

When we continued our tour, Michele had started to hear people yelling at her, and she said a lot of people had come to that location for emergencies. Linda nodded and told us that the police used this location to practise emergency response training exercises. Michele sensed the presence of a man and told Linda the name she picked up. Linda confirmed that he was a long-term, dedicated employee who had died a few years before.

Linda then took us down to the women's washroom. There are two washrooms on either side of the stairs. After a brief check of the areas, there was nothing that required further investigation down there.

"This is odd. I'm getting images of children's parties with balloons," Michele told us. Linda confirmed that the building had been used for children's parties in the past, since there is a large room used as a dining hall.

Later, during a break, Sheryl, Linda, and Michele were standing by the side entrance when Sheryl was suddenly overwhelmed by the strong scent of pineapple. "Did someone just put on hand cream or use soap that smells like pineapple?" she asked. Everyone said no. She kept sniffing, trying to locate the source. Finally we all started to smell it. We kept searching but could not find a source.

After our break we walked towards the stairs and noticed that several of the presidential photos were crooked. Michele was the first to notice this and started taking photos. Unfortunately, we had no photos from our initial walkthrough to prove the portraits had indeed moved, but we all knew those pictures were not crooked before.

Paul went upstairs to put the recording system in one of the rooms, and I headed outside to get some exterior photos of the building. Michele, Linda, and Sheryl went back to the room Linda had said she didn't like to work in. Michele and Sheryl immediately experienced extreme dizziness and had to sit down. Michele started to feel like she couldn't breathe and Sheryl started feeling like her head was being crushed in a vice. Michele reported that she was seeing what she described as an old black-and-white film running in her head. She said she could hear that noise that an old reel makes when the film has run out. As they sat there Sheryl mentioned that the pineapple smell had returned, and eventually Michele and Linda smelled it too.

Michele picked up the name "Marjorie" or "Marge," and suddenly the bad atmosphere cleared and the pressure and dizziness faded away. Sheryl wondered if the pineapple smell had something to do with it.

Paul and I joined the rest of the team and continued on the tour, stopping in the president's office. As we stood there quietly, we heard consecutive knocks in the far left corner of the room. Everyone remained quiet, and Michele asked out loud for them to repeat the sound. Michele called Sheryl over to where she was standing and asked if she could smell men's cologne. Sheryl moved across the room, and indeed she detected the smell. We tried again to make contact with whoever was in the room, but we got no response.

Michele told us that there was a residue of the people who had worked here, not just one specific individual. Sheryl was getting waves of dizziness again. Michele reported hearing a dog bark and said she was shown a car accident. "Accidents seem to happen to the people that work in this office," she said. She also reported hearing a man's voice. "He wanders. He's not from this room." There was originally a man that was suicidal, and he was part of the spirit energy from this area. "Kind of a little psycho," Michele said. She was picking up the name "Kenneth" as well as the name "Jacob." All of a sudden, Michele was touched on her hair and arm. She bolted from the chair and told him to stop. "It's like hide and seek with him." Then she said, "Something Black. I'm here, I'm there, I'm everywhere!"

I led the team further down the hall. Michele heard more than one person talking. We entered the general manager's office, and she said she got a good feeling from the office, so we paused for a few moments. Michele sensed a "gathering room" and felt a lot of people around. Sheryl started smelling pineapple again.

We moved into the upstairs staff lounge and kitchen area. The door from the kitchen was now open, but this was the door we had closed earlier to keep the noise from the coolers away from our camera. Suddenly Michele exclaimed "Ralph!" very loudly. She thought that someone, possibly an ex-security employee, had opened the door.

We decided to move into the centre of the floor and sit quietly. Michele and Sheryl headed off to use the bathroom on the second floor. Michele had left the bathroom door open the last time she had been in that room, but it was shut. The group tested the door by opening it again to see if it would shut on its own, but it remained open.

They returned and the five of us sat quietly for a while. Nothing happened, so we decided to take a break. Michele, Linda, and Sheryl were standing by the side entrance just inside the office area, and Paul and I were outside. Michele told them that she kept hearing Paul's name being called out.

Michele had to use the bathroom. Linda pointed out that there was a private washroom adjacent to the exit door. As Michele entered, she saw a woman standing inside. She said that the woman looked like a librarian, because she had her hair in a tight bun and was wearing a white blouse and a long black skirt. She had a very stern look on her face and was not happy about Michele being in there. Michele called Sheryl over so that she could experience the atmosphere of the room and give some feedback. Sheryl pushed open the door and felt a very strong sense of someone rushing towards her to push her away. Sheryl bolted from the room. "I have never felt anything that strongly before, I can't go in there."

Paul and I were told what had happened, so we decided to go in too. Sheryl remained in the hallway. Michele started to describe a scowling woman wearing old-fashioned 1920s clothing. Paul tried to make contact by asking her to make a noise if she wanted us to leave the room. Michele heard "Hogwash."

"Who uses the word 'hogwash'?" she said, laughing. She then heard the name "Stella" and "Get out, get out."

Paul again asked for contact of some sort but there was none. We waited for a few more moments but all remained quiet, so everyone left.

We decided to go back upstairs so that Michele could sit in the main foyer and try to make contact. I grabbed a chair and placed it in the middle of the big open area. Michele sat down and we waited silently. She asked for any spirit in the building to come and speak with her. "Some stay, some wander," she said. She called out to the man she'd seen earlier at the top of the stairs. She asked him to talk to her. Nothing. She then asked the woman from the downstairs washroom. Michele said the woman was telling her that we didn't belong here. She also kept hearing the name or word "Duclough."

Paul and I were hearing noises from downstairs, and we kept peering over the banister.

"They're coming," Michele said. "They're not harmful." Then she said "Black shoes."

My heart almost skipped a beat when I saw through a reflection in the window two legs with black shoes pass in the hallway on the lower floor. Paul and I raced down to the first floor, with the rest of the team following us. There we came face to face with a maintenance person doing scheduled building rounds.

We went back upstairs and sat quietly for a while, but nothing more happened. It was time to pack up, but as we did so there was a thud from down the hall. We moved off to investigate and found that the lights were now on in the Queen's bathroom.

We packed up and went home. Paul and I discussed the building, and although we had noticed a few strange things, we believed it was a relatively quiet place. He called me a few days later to look at the surveillance.

SURVEILLANCE RESULTS

On the upper floor system a male EVP called out "Cathy … *bang* … Cathy … *big bang.*"

Another male EVP said "Edit it," followed by unidentifiable whispers.

As we returned to the second floor, a male EVP said "Upstairs now."

A female EVP said "Hal," then all went quiet.

When we had returned from one of our breaks, the team arrived at the top of the stairs and a male EVP said "Get out."

During Michele's question period, she looked at me and said, "Not getting anything." Just after, a male EVP was recorded saying "Ask me now."

During our second floor tour, Paul's cell phone rang, and he walked away from the rest of the team. As he passed the camera, a male EVP was recorded: "I'm now talking … hang up."

Later a male EVP said, "Out of … the way."

The camera near the lunchroom captured the sound of a spoon tinkling in a coffee mug then two distinct taps. Near the camera, the floor squeaked and there was the sound of walking and a door opening.

Paul came around the corner taking photos, and a male EVP said "Get out … from here."

I now looked at Paul. "Guess I couldn't have been more wrong." The place appeared to be a lot more active than we realized. The next day I called to arrange another visit to the Press Building.

Eleventh Investigation

Press Building
June 2010

Paul, Sheryl, Christina, and Me

For this visit we kept the team small. We placed one camera on the main floor, hidden amongst some filing cabinets, and a second camera on the upper floor in the main hall facing the grand staircase. We then spent a long time on the second floor. Our surveillance equipment did not record anything out of the ordinary on the main floor.

After setting the system to record, we made our way to the lounge area. EVPs were immediately recorded.

A male voice said "Henry" once, then again after a long pause.

Another male voice replied, "Yes."

As the camera recorded us turning the corner near the top of the stairs, a male EVP said "They're coming."

The team went down to the main floor, but the activity continued upstairs.

There was a distinct tapping sound near the camera, and a male EVP said "Cathy."

A female voice replied, "Yes."

The lights dimmed momentarily, then brightened again. This was the same phenomenon we had observed in the archives.

A male EVP called "Cathy ... Cathy ... come here." There was a very loud bang and the lights dimmed again.

As we returned to the floor, the lights brightened. The team approached the camera and started asking questions. We received no response until Christina asked, "Are you press?" An EVP replied, but it could not be deciphered.

We continued our tour of the building but found nothing unusual. When we arrived at the large open space directly in front of the camera, as Sheryl and I talked there was whispering around us. Paul came over and told us that the coffee had given him heartburn, and a female EVP said, "Yeah, that's me."

While we still got some interesting data, the second visit seemed to have been a great deal quieter and produced less than the first visit.

New Reports

Throughout our investigations, we kept hearing about new incidents at the General Services Building.

At 1:50 a.m. one night, a security officer stationed at the General Services building noticed a tall figure passing behind his coworker. She reported a icy shiver along her spine. It moved off and left the building via the main south door. He described the figure as male, and although he didn't see its face, he did see it from the side and the back. The officer reported that it had thick, curly short hair, but the colour was difficult to determine. It was wearing a trench coat that was a flat blue with pale blue vinyl edging around the outside. It appeared that the figure was either seven feet tall or was floating above the floor.

We wanted to go back for another look, but time constraints dictated that we keep to our schedule — there was so much to do and so little time.

Twelfth Investigation

Civic Arena
July 2010

Paul, Michele, Peter, Amanda, Darrin, Jennifer, Christina, and Me

The Civic Arena opened on December 16, 1921 and was shared by the Canadian National Exhibition and the Royal Agricultural Winter Fair. From 1942 to 1945 the building was used as a training base for the Canadian Army named "Manning Depot #1 Toronto." There were five manning depots. The other four were located in Brandon, Edmonton, Quebec City, and Lachine.

We were told that there was strange activity occurring within the building and that we should have a look. Paul, Sheryl, Christina, and I went for a tour to see what was going on.

Christina led us to the side door, where we entered a maintenance area. We walked through the large room to a ramp used by the Zamboni when entering the cavernous rink.

The team was inspecting the area when Paul saw a shadow either run or move very quickly past a large opening at the opposite side of the stands. It wasn't long before everyone started to notice solid black shadows that seemed to appear from nowhere and rush past a doorway or support column, only to disappear into the darkness. We could feel them watching us, and there was no doubt that they were there. What we didn't know was their intention. We speculated that they could be curious about what we were up to, or possibly they were protective of the property.

Courtesy Exhibition Place Archives

The Coliseum opened on December 16, 1921.

I spoke to Paul about some of the challenges we faced in this building. The sheer size would be a problem, and the low hum of the ventilation system could make obtaining EVPs difficult.

After our tour, we started making arrangements to come back and do a full investigation.

The team met up with Christina, and she introduced us to Jennifer Foster, an employee who wanted to participate in our investigation to see exactly what we do. I told her she would most likely have an experience that night. I didn't tell her this to frighten her, but in my experience those who are new to ghost investigations seem to have more experiences.

We placed our equipment near the door and led the team on a quick tour. When we were done we placed a night vision camera in the arena and an audio/video surveillance camera at the top of the ramp looking into the maintenance area.

We headed off on our walkthrough with Michele leading the group. The building was so hot, it was almost unbearable as we made our way along rear corridors and common areas with rows of empty concession stands.

"There is a lot going on here — a lot of activity," Michele said, pausing in the hallway. "There is a man over there near the concession stand." We couldn't see anything unusual, but several of us took photographs of the area. "I get the name Stanley." She stopped again. "There's a horse, why would there be a horse here?" Again we saw nothing. "There is polter-geist activity in here, definitely. Oh, I just heard an evil laugh!"

Peter captured on his digital recorder a growl-like noise and several seconds of indistinguishable whispering.

We went into the arena through a massive doorway and noticed a strange light in one of the upper seating boxes. It had not been present earlier. I asked Christina if she would take us to the upper levels. As we climbed the stairs, there were strange noises and banging from below. Each time we paused, and each time we saw nothing.

We headed for the stairs to the upper deck, which houses private seating boxes and offices. We stopped, and this time, despite the unbear-able heat, we were faced with an icy cold spot directly in our path. We searched for a vent or a fan or other source to explain why this small cold column stood in our way, but we could find nothing. It lasted a few moments then was consumed by the heat and was gone.

Peter's digital recorded a deep inhale and exhale.

Michele led onward towards the stairs. As we walked through the hall, she halted. "There is a very tall man walking quickly towards us." No one else on the team perceived him. Michele stepped back against the wall as if to allow someone to pass her. "Can't you see him? He has grey-ing hair and he's wearing scruffy clothing." She described his size and said he bore a resemblance to the character of John Coffey in the movie *The Green Mile*, portrayed by actor Michael Clarke Duncan. She thought his name was Taley, Towie, or Tally.

Meanwhile, while we were upstairs the camera in the maintenance area recorded the sound of heavy footsteps on the ramp. An EVP was captured of a male voice saying something unknown.

Amanda noticed dimes were strewn all over the floor in the hallway and thought it strange, but we paid little attention and continued on to the lit private box. The door was locked, so Paul knocked. We monitored it for a few minutes, but nothing happened, and there were no sounds from inside the room.

As we started back towards the stairs, Peter recorded a distorted "Hello" and a quick laugh. No one heard it at the time.

As we headed down to the ground floor, back into that thick and heavy heat, the team's mood started to lighten. Someone said it was so hot, we desperately wanted to find that cold spot again. It was suggested we create a T-shirt saying "Stay cool this summer, hug a ghost."

Amanda noticed that the camera monitor showed nothing but snow. Paul checked the system and called me over. Someone had switched the input channel, effectively shutting down surveillance on this unit.

I reset the system and began recording again, then the team headed outside for a break and some fresh air.

As we stepped outside, it was like walking out of a furnace — the heat inside that building made every task a chore.

While we were outside, the system recorded the sound of something falling and hitting the floor, then an EVP, gender unknown, saying "I'll save it."

We re-entered the building, and I jokingly said, "Well, I think I'm going to test the investigative skills of my team and see if you can find a working vending machine."

The camera recorded an EVP of a male saying "Great."

Jennifer said that she knew where one was, so she took the lead. Behind us the camera recorded a shadow moving across the wall. It appeared to be following us down into the arena. We crossed the arena then back up into the common area. As we moved through the corridors, team members reported seeing quick shadows darting around the doorways.

Michele stopped. "There is a man in blue coveralls kneeling down working on something. I can't see what it is."

No one else could see what she was describing, but Peter's digital recorded an EVP of a male voice saying "Come on."

Like an oasis shimmering in the burning desert sun, the vending machine lay ahead of us. We bought ice-cold water and returned to the arena.

The team split up into small groups, taking up vantage points around the arena. I climbed higher and sat down for a commanding view — from this point I could see everyone taking positions in the stands, with the exception of Darrin who was walking around filming.

Only a few minutes had passed when Paul signaled to me. I had started down to where he was when he motioned me to go the long way around. I followed his direction and came up behind him. He pointed to the front seating box adjacent to the floor of the arena. "Listen."

I stood with him silently, straining to hear. A sound came from that section that sounded like someone shifting in a seat and aluminum scraping on concrete. I looked at him. "I've heard that a few times now," he whispered.

I walked over to the box. As I stepped into it, the aluminum base scraped against the concrete floor. I could see nothing unusual inside the box, so I looked over my shoulder at Paul. He nodded to indicate that it was the same sound. I took a seat and waited for something else to happen, but nothing did.

Peter recorded "Hey!"

The camera in the maintenance area was still recording, and it picked up a small yellow ball of light that seemed to come from the wall. The light stayed for a few minutes then faded away, coming back larger a few moments later. After a couple of minutes, it too faded back into the darkness. It soon returned even bigger, elongated, and jagged. The yellow light eventually dissolved away into blackness. No source was ever found, and what it was remains a mystery.

Michele and Peter sat together. He using his digital recorder.

"Do you hear singing?" Michele asked.

"No."

"Let us know you are here, make a noise." There was a faint sound near them. "I am hearing a Judy or Julie, she is standing over my right shoulder."

Peter's recorder captured a whispered "Ju …"

"The surname is Anderson ... Henderson. She has an accent, pronounced HANderson. She looks all dolled-up for an event. She has a long skirt tight around the waist, a white blouse, and a large-brimmed hat. She doesn't look like she is from this era. She has blonde hair, she has an accent."

"American?" Peter asked.

"Yeah, it has a twang to it."

"Where are you from?" he said.

"Georgia. She was born here, but she comes from Georgia."

"Do you have family here?" Peter asked.

"Her mama's side, her daddy was from the States."

"What year is it?"

"1923."

No further contact was made with that spirit.

Christina and Jennifer were sitting a few rows back when Jennifer felt a soft touch on her left cheek and neck, then a few moments later a touch on her right forearm. Christina noticed a shadow crossing behind them that was followed by a cool breeze. Jennifer was flooded with emotions that were not her own — she had no idea why she was crying.

The camera in the maintenance area recorded heavy footfalls and something falling to the floor with a clang. A male EVP said "Damn it."

There was movement around the camera, rustling, then something fell or was dropped again. A male EVP said "Crap!" Then all was quiet.

The team started to assemble around Christina and Jennifer to find out what was going on. "What happened?" Paul asked.

They explained what had occurred and Jennifer mentioned her eyes watering.

"That's what happens. In a lot of these encounters, your eyes will water for no reason," Paul told her.

Amanda was still sitting quietly some distance from us when a hissing noise just to her left startled her. She looked towards the sound and saw two black shadows shooting downwards over the seats, heading towards the centre of the arena. They weren't upright and seemed to be moving forward horizontally. They vanished into the darkness. Amanda quickly made her way back to the team.

Our time was just about up, so we decided to start packing. This was one of the most haunted buildings we had encountered on the grounds, and the entire team had experienced strange phenomena. As we were putting away the camera equipment, I was asked how many spirits might be dwelling here in this building, and after considering each event, I said it would be impossible to even hazard a guess.

It was not until later that night, when Amanda got home and kicked off her shoes, that she noticed a shiny dime in the bottom of her running shoe. She was at a loss to explain how it could have gotten in there.

Thirteenth Investigation

General Services Building and Queen Elizabeth Buildings
July 2010

Paul, Sheryl, Jim, Anna, Christina, and Me

Our focus on this night would be the Queen Elizabeth Building, but some of our team was running late, so we decided to spend some time in the General Services Building. Christina met us in the parking lot. We decided to walk around the building.

As we walked in silence, my thoughts drifted to a fateful night I'd read about, way back in 1912. Two men, Eli Dunkleman and Joseph Rosenthal, were lured behind the hydro station, and something terrible happened — Dunkelman suffered a fractured skull, and Rosenthal's body was found with a rope around his neck and his skull crushed by a rock. Dunkelman survived and blamed a man named Charlie Gibson. Gibson was tried and sentenced to hang, but he had an alibi for that night and wrote to the media. Rumours circulated about five men being involved and about two named "Alf" and "Red" being the real killers, but no evidence surfaced. Due to public pressure, Gibson's sentence was lowered to life in prison, but not long afterward a prominent businessman came forward and said that he had met two men named Alf and Red in British Columbia. They knew all about the Gibson case.

I wondered, was it Rosenthal's traumatic death that tethered his poor soul to this place? I stopped and looked up at the high-voltage towers. Could the energy there play a part in keeping them around, beckoning spirits like a moth to a flame? Then a thought struck me that made me feel colder — what was so terrifying out there in the dark that even insects seek refuge around the porch light?

I made an extremely disturbing discovery while conducting historical research on the area. I discovered that a very small patch of ground behind the General Services Building had a long history of luring people to their deaths. Between 1884 and 1916, numerous deaths have been recorded there. One of the strangest incidents occurred on July 4, 1906. A man riding a Grand Trunk train from Buffalo to Toronto's Union Station fell off the train. He had apparently felt ill and stepped out onto the platform between cars to get some fresh air. When the train arrived at Union Station, the man's friends discovered he was missing and reported it to the authorities. They backtracked up the line and discovered his body a short distance west of Strachan Avenue, behind the General Services Building.

I looked out past the construction materials, past the high chain-link fence, to that patch of ground that had claimed so many lives. Was there something out there looking back at me? The thought made me shudder. I wasn't about to tempt fate, so I led the team to the back door.

We entered the building and walked the long hallway. Could spirits possibly manifest so perfectly here that we might see them and think that they are just other employees going about their daily business? Anything seemed possible within the energy of this building.

We stopped outside the freight elevator. I had asked Christina if we could go to the basement. When we filed in, Sheryl sad a heavy, oppressive feeling immediately came over her.

As we stepped out into the basement, she started to feel as if she were being suffocated. She paused for a moment then pushed on into the depths.

We moved over to the gated area and looked around, taking pictures. I was facing Paul, who had his back to the gate. I was caught off-guard when what I'd thought was Paul's shadow peeled away, moved quickly beyond the gate, and vanished.

I moved in and started taking photos, all of which showed nothing remarkable.

Paul noticed a small, blinking light about the size of a dime moving around my legs, then it vanished as well.

The team explored the basement for a few more minutes then took the elevator up to the top floor to investigate the archives.

Christina led us through the main office and into the stacks. It felt good being back here, exhilarating, since you never knew what you might see around the next corner.

Unfortunately, it was time to move on. We had to meet a few more people and go to another location. Christina locked up, and we headed down to our cars.

THE QUEEN ELIZABETH BUILDING

As we pulled up, we met Jim and Anna and entered the Queen Elizabeth Building.

It was getting late when we entered. We dropped our equipment near the door and decided to tour the building first to get a feel for the layout, and see if we could detect any potential activity.

The floor was divided up into offices and cubicles. We started our tour along the perimeter hallways. Everything seemed quiet and normal for a few minutes. Then Sheryl reported feeling heaviness and a headache, and a moment later Jim complained of feeling dizzy. I moved to Paul and told him that we should place some of our surveillance equipment in this hallway. I didn't know if what was being reported was simply coincidence, environmental, or something paranormal — the only way to be sure was to get the equipment up and running. That's when we heard the whine of a vacuum cleaner. A cleaner was scheduled to be there for a few more hours. Her presence on the floor would render our surveillance useless, so Christina suggested that we go to the upper floor and dining hall.

Most of the team took the stairs to the upper floor, and Paul and I moved the equipment by elevator. We unloaded and placed one surveillance unit at the back of the dining room and another at the front, facing each other. The team split up and began to investigate the floor.

Courtesy Exhibition Place Archives

The Queen Elizabeth Building is an unremarkable two-storey structure built in 1957 and was originally opened as the Women's Building.

Sheryl moved to the rear of the room, where there was a bar. She felt a male presence there. She moved around the bar and immediately felt unwelcome. The feeling was so strong that she moved away.

Jim and Paul were standing near the doorway. They could hear walking and shuffling sounds near the front of the dining hall, but there was no one around.

Anna took the parabolic microphone and went to the washrooms. She had entered the women's washroom by herself and was standing quietly when she was startled by a sudden rush of water from the faucet. She left the washroom and called everyone over. Paul, Sheryl, and came in with Anna. She explained that she'd been standing next to the middle toilet stall with her hand on its door when the faucet started. Paul checked the sink and discovered the faucets were controlled by motion detectors. We moved back to the door and asked Anna to stand where she had been when the incident occurred — when she did, she was too far away to have triggered the motion detector. Paul asked her to move closer and closer to the sink until the motion turned the water on — she had to stand right in front of the sink to make this happen.

Everyone moved out into the foyer. Sheryl was the last one out of the bathroom. She said, "There is a female in there."

Paul handed Anna a voice recorder and asked her to go back. Everyone stood quietly waiting.

She went to the centre of the room and started asking questions. "Is there anyone here? Did you turn on the water?" She heard a whisper and felt a cold breeze on her face. She went out into the foyer but left the voice recorder on the counter. She looked terrified. I heard a sound from inside the bathroom and motioned to everyone to be quiet. The sound came again, like a rubber sneaker shoe on tiles. We entered and saw nothing.

We checked the voice recorder, finding some odd noises then an EVP. It was a young male voice: "Bullshit."

We were told by security that the space had been booked for business this evening. There was a slight mix-up in the scheduling. When you're dealing with a large company, these things will happen. The team quickly packed up, and we made our way back outside. As we stood in the parking lot, we discussed the evening's events. We decided to try again later.

SURVEILLANCE RESULTS

Over the next few days Paul reviewed and analyzed the surveillance recordings. He was very excited when he called me.

It was interesting to note that Sheryl had felt a man near the bar area and that Paul and Jim had felt a female.

A female EVP was recorded saying "Benny."

A male EVP said "What, Merriam?"

A female is heard saying "*unknown word*, ya, ya."

Another female EVP said "Benny, Benny."

There was a long pause, then a female EVP said "Easy, Benny."

A short while later Anna went alone into the dining room. She swept the area with the parabolic microphone. She didn't hear what was being recorded, a female EVP calling "Benny, Benny."

There was a loud, indescribable sound that Anna must have heard, since it caused her to stop in her tracks. She moved among the chairs towards the exit then stopped again. A female EVP said, "Yes, we are dead."

A male voice said, "Check them out."

Anna left the room. Although she had reported hearing some sounds in the dining area, she had not heard these voices. The room was empty as an older-sounding male EVP said, "Out."

A few minutes later Paul entered the room, and a female EVP was recorded saying "Benny."

Jim entered the room. He took a random seat and sat quietly while Paul walked around.

"It's very cold here," Jim said.

Paul walked over to Jim and noticed that that smaller area was considerably cooler. "Yes, it is."

An enormous bang was heard that startled both Jim and Paul. They went to investigate but found no source.

A female EVP said "Benny, come here."

That was the end of our recording session.

The 131st Canadian National Exhibition

It was the 2010 opening of the CNE, and I was asked to give some lectures on the work we were doing on the grounds. I recruited Paul, Amanda, and Sheryl to participate. The idea was we would give the ghost lectures and then people could enjoy a ghost tour hosted by Records and Archives, Exhibition Place. It was very exciting to see record crowds attending both. Although the public shared a lot of interesting ghost stories with us, only two people brought forth information that related directly to Exhibition Place. The first was a story from a patron, the other a photo taken by a gentleman on one of the ghost tours.

Tony Aronis was making his way through the crowd after a long day at the Ex when a man came out of nowhere and stopped directly in his path. Mr. Aronis described the man as very pale, unshaven, with a head full of grey hair. He stared wild-eyed at Mr. Aronis and said, "This place is haunted!"

Mr. Aronis asked, "What place?"

"There!" the man replied, pointing to the Horse Palace.

Mr. Aronis glanced over to see where the man had pointed. When he looked back, the man was gone.

On another ghost walking tour in August 2010, Peter S. Dzivy was taking random photos in the Horse Palace when he captured what appears to be the ghostly image of someone walking a horse on

Courtesy Exhibition Place Archives

A partial view of the Princes' Gates.

the main floor of the building. Mr. Dzivy said he didn't see anything unusual at the time and only noticed the image when reviewing his pictures the next day.

Meanwhile, ghost reports were still coming in from the General Services Building, and as much as I enjoyed doing the ghost lectures, I was itching to get back to the investigations.

Courtesy Peter S. Dzi:y

In this photo from a ghost tour of the Horse Palace, a ghostly image of someone walking a horse can be seen.

In the new addition to the second floor of the General Services Building, a member of the protection services team caught a glimpse of a figure near the washrooms. It was a tall man standing sideways looking back at him. The figure was silver/white and seemed to shimmer. As soon as they locked eyes, the image vanished. This was the same place where another member of the protection services team had seen the figure of a man a few days before. Notably, several months before, a security officer using the washroom was disturbed by knocks on the door when no one else was on the floor.

Possibly the Most Haunted Building

The Crystal Palace was built in 1858 and was originally located on the north side of King Street at Shaw Avenue. It was moved to the fairgrounds in 1878, and in 1906 it burned to the ground.

In 1907, the Horticulture Building was erected on its location. It was designed by George W. Gouinlock.

WORKER PLUMMETS TO HIS DEATH

On November 6, 1902, Charles M., an ironworker labouring atop of the Crystal Palace, fell to his death at the Exhibition Grounds.

THE SS *NORONIC*

The SS *Noronic*, nicknamed "Queen of the Lakes," was launched in 1913 in Port Arthur, Ontario. At 362 feet long, the ship had five decks and could carry as many as 600 passengers and 200 crew members. On September 14, 1949, the *Noronic* set out from Detroit, Michigan on a seven-day pleasure cruise of Lake Ontario. It was carrying 524 passengers and 171 crew as it slipped into Pier 9 in Toronto Harbour for an overnight stay. In the early hours of September 16, fire broke out in a starboard linen closet on C deck. It took eight minutes from first discovery of the fire to the sounding of the alarm, and by that time

The Crystal Palace

A temporary morgue was set up in the Horticultural Building for the victims of the *Noronic* fire.

most of the decks were on fire. What resulted was absolute panic, since most passengers on the upper decks were not aware of the fire until it was too late. Of the five towering decks, the only access to the dock was from the lowest one. By then all the stairways, which were made of wood, were ablaze. By early morning, 139 people had died — all of them passengers and most of them American. All of the crew made it safely off the ship.

As the House of Commons launched an investigation, and the bodies of the dead were collected and sent to a makeshift morgue located in the Horticulture Building at Exhibition Place.

The high mortality rate was blamed on the cowardice of the crew and the fact that the fire hoses were out of service. The cause was never discovered. As a side note, the *Noronic's* sister ship, the SS *Hamonic*, burned in 1945 without any loss of life.

THE FLOOD

An alarm alerted security of a flood in the Horticulture Building, and an officer responded immediately. He arrived at the secure and empty building, noting that the alarm was in the basement. He arrived at the room to find it locked. He used his pass key to enter, to find a water valve had been turned on, allowing water to quickly fill the room.

The police and fire department arrived and met him in the basement. The fire team noted that the valve required a special piece of equipment to open and close it, called a church key. They could not explain how the valve could have been opened without this piece of equipment, in a locked room in a locked building in the middle of the night.

After the scene was cleaned up and secured, the police and firefighters left.

The security officer worked his way back up to the main floor, locking doors as he went. As he was making his way to the exit, he heard a noise from the exterior door, as though someone were trying to force it open. He was unnerved and charged the door. He kicked the crash bar and the door flew open. Stepping out into the night air, he could see in all directions, but there was no one around.

He returned to the security office, only to learn that this night was the anniversary of the 1949 *Noronic* fire.

Discovery

Paul had discovered something interesting while analyzing the audio surveillance. He kept his findings quiet for a long time because he wanted to be sure of what he had found. He called me and told me we needed to discuss something, so we met at a local coffee shop.

"I found something."

"What have you got?" I asked.

"Remember Danny from the archives?"

"The bell ringer? Yeah, why?"

"He is following us to just about every job. He keeps turning up on our tapes."

I thought about that for a moment. "What do you mean just about every job? So there are investigations that he stays away from?"

"I noticed that he is at a lot of our investigations. With his bells and called by name."

"Do you have the dates for each time we detected him?"

"Yes."

It took some figuring out, but there was a pattern. Every time Christina came out with us and started off at the General Services Building, Danny would end up on our surveillance. On investigations where Christina was absent, Danny seemed to be absent as well.

I called Christina and told her our theory. She stunned me when she said she thought that something from the archives was following her around.

Fourteenth Investigation

Cemetery
September 2010

Paul, Amanda, Christina, and Me

During the American assault on York, 130 men died from both sides. Most were buried in shallow graves, some covered by only inches of earth.

In one incident, a mobile magazine exploded, killing twenty men. British troops took refuge in a ravine north of the fort. They knew the fort would be lost and deliberately caused the powder magazine to explode, causing massive losses to the advancing Americans. Thirty-eight men were killed, including Zebulon Pike, who was leading the advance, and 222 were wounded. The dead were either buried in a mass grave or where they fell. Others who were killed while fighting were also buried where they fell. In 1860, the remains of fifteen soldiers were discovered in a trench near Bathurst and Front Streets.

A military cemetery was established just inside the present-day Dufferin Gates, but the cemetery was moved due to the extremely poor soil. Its present location is east of Strachan Avenue.

Although there are numerous estimates of how many people are interred in this cemetery, the actual number is unknown. The first burial here was in 1863, when the British turned Stanley Barracks over to the Canadian government. After 1870, the cemetery fell into neglect. It wasn't until 1921, when a *Toronto Star* article stated that the cemetery was in a pitiful state, that something was finally done.

—/—

Paul, Amanda, and I met with Christina at the General Services Building parking lot and made our way by foot up Strachan Avenue to the cemetery on the east side of the street. The sun was sitting low on the horizon and it was windy and cool when we began our descent down into the grounds. We assembled at the wall of tombstones in the centre of the park. The group split up to investigate — Paul and I moved along the northern boundary as Amanda skirted the southern fence line. A man was playing fetch with his dogs, a young couple made out near some pines, and there was litter and graffiti everywhere.

It was interesting to note that as the sun went down, all pedestrian traffic through the cemetery stopped.

Amanda reported feeling the ground vibrating beneath her feet as she walked through the centre of the cemetery.

We talked about the history of the cemetery and the War of 1812. I thought that since witnesses had reported seeing spectral soldiers amongst the trees looking towards the lake, it was possible that this had been the escape route when the British fled the fort after blowing up the powder magazine. How many fell on this patch of ground during that conflict? Looking towards the fort, it is easy to see this place as a battleground, a place where many fell and many soldiers were buried after the battle. This place should have been hallowed ground for the soldiers who had died and were buried where they had fallen. Instead, the place was forgotten and overgrown until 1863, when it became a military cemetery. We wondered if those soldiers felt the injustice of laying down their lives and not being honoured, basically shoved aside, their resting places disturbed or even desecrated so that others could be laid to rest.

Even though the memorial wall has a simple plaque stating "Military Cemetery," there is no acknowledgement of what went on here during the War of 1812. This, for the spirits here, compounds the lack of respect and perceived injustice.

The sun had gone and night surrounded us. Paul and Christina took turns scanning the cemetery with night vision equipment, and Amanda and I took photos of the southern tree line. Paul noticed a man standing against a tree at the far end of the park, but as he looked without the night scope, the man was not visible. Christina also looked through the scope and also saw the man, but without the scope no one was visible. Upon further investigation, they discovered that no one was in the area.

The team broke up and photographed all areas of the park. Paul and Amanda stopped by the southern tree line, and I was a few feet away when Paul called out, "Something just hit me in the back."

Amanda and Paul were searching the grass when I arrived. The beam of a flashlight danced off something lying on the grass, and Paul and I both fell to our knees for a closer inspection. It was a brassy coin.

Paul picked it up. It was a half penny token dated 1812. This was spectacular. Everyone was amazed at how a piece of history could materialize out of thin air. Paul rolled the coin over. On the reverse was Lady Justice, sporting her blindfold and scales. This was poignant in light of our discussion about the cemetery and injustice. Some believe that items can be transferred from one location to another by means not yet understood by modern science, and in this particular case an item not only moved locations but also from one time to another. The coin was handed to Christina for safekeeping.

Amanda took the night scope and started investigating the tree line. I moved along the trees and took photographs. Amanda called out that she had seen a person standing on a hillock who turned, took a few steps then vanished. We went to the spot and found an old fence covered in vines and leaves fifteen feet above the gully that was the old Grand Trunk rail lines. We saw no one, so we split up. Amanda moved back out to the lawn and I moved between the trees. I felt a hand grasp my arm. Although I knew it was a hand, my brain told me it was not possible, since there was no one near me. I tried to rationalize it and looked for a tree branch that might have snagged me, but there was nothing. I pulled my arm away, and whatever it was released me. I turned all around, searching for an explanation, but found none. I moved back out onto the lawn.

We spent the next half hour touring and photographing the cemetery then headed over to the arena for another investigation there.

THE COIN

The coin appears to be a Breton 960 Lower Canada 1812 Tiffin Half Penny token. These were made of copper and weighed between 8.2 and 8.6 grams.

On the obverse is a bust of King George III surrounded by a wreath. On the reverse is an image of Britannia, who symbolizes British patriotism, and on this particular coin she is holding the scales of justice. The coin was designed and struck by Thomas Holliday.

The hole punched through the coin was most likely so it could be worn as a necklace, although one historian did tell me that soldiers' uniforms were in such bad condition back then that they punched holes in their coins and tied them on a string around their wrist so they wouldn't lose them.

The obverse side (left) and reverse side (right) of the coin that hit Paul's back.

Fifteenth Investigation

Civic Arena
September 2010

Paul, Amanda, Christina,
Security and Operations Employees, and Me

Someone reported that a phone in one of the suites in the Civic Arena often rang, and when it was answered, there was no one on the other end. One day when it rang, the person answering noticed that it was not connected to the wall jack. Our main mission on this night would be to investigate that phone.

Led by security, we entered the darkened building to meet up with an employee who was working late. They led us through the service corridor past the Zamboni parking garage to the storage and maintenance area where we had placed one of our cameras on the previous visit. Paul suggested that since we had recorded activity in this area before, it would be an ideal location for a camera placement on this visit as well. As I set up the audio/video surveillance system, Paul explored the vast area nearby. He saw a black figure of a person run past the wall and vanish. As he walked over to investigate, he saw an ad on the wall and laughed — the poster, completely unrelated to anything paranormal, had the line "Feel the Spirit." As I approached him, he turned and said, "I just saw something run down there." We stood for a moment watching and listening but saw and heard nothing more.

The team was ready now, and with security in the lead, we started off. We headed down the main hall, past empty concession stands, heading upstairs to the mysterious ringing phone. Security opened the office.

I quickly confirmed that the phone was indeed dead. We settled down, waiting for something to happen.

The office was large and open to the arena below. There was a feeling amongst some of us that someone had fallen from the third floor. The operations worker said that was funny, as he had thought the same thing the day before our arrival. Apparently, some time before our work at Exhibition Place, two workers were finishing a late shift when a tiered response of police, fire, and ambulance workers arrived at the building. They had received an emergency call from the office about someone in dire trouble. The two workers were the only ones in the building, and all the offices were found vacant and secure.

As Amanda, Christina, and I stood around waiting, we heard a very clear and distinct groan of pain from just below the office — it sounded as if a man was somewhere below us and in great agony. We looked at each other. We looked over the balcony and scanned down with our flashlights, but nothing was there.

I went for a closer look. Paul pointed to the far wall across the arena near the main staircase and told Christina that there was an odd light hovering there. She saw it too, and they watched as the light faded in and out. It moved very quickly and was followed by a large shadow along the wall. Both descended the main stairs out of view.

I told the team that we were moving out. We needed to go to where the activity was. Security led the way, and we started down the hall to the stairs, moving to the walkway below the office.

That phone didn't ring, at least not for us.

Christina and I took the lead along the walkway towards the main stairs, where we had seen the shadow. A loud groan stopped us in our tracks. The creepy sound echoed again, but we could not determine its source. We stood for several minutes waiting for it to reoccur, but all remained quiet.

We continued on to the main stairs, stopping near a mechanical room. The operations person had told us that many years before, near where we were standing, a mechanical room had flooded. Somehow a valve had been turned on. The valve was turned past its limit and was extremely difficult to shut off. A security person then told us about fire sprinklers activating in this area and flooding the floor, but no cause was ever found.

We toured the building for another half hour, but nothing out of the ordinary was noted. We called it a night and packed up.

Paul called a few days later and told me that nothing had been captured on our surveillance equipment.

Sixteenth Investigation

Cemetery
October 2010

Michelle, Sarah, Helen, Roula, Ron, Jonathan, Paul, Amanda, and Me

We arrived as the sun set on the horizon and took the short walk to the cemetery. I had assembled a group of people who had never been to the cemetery as observers — the majority had never been on a ghost investigation at all — interspersed with a few veterans of paranormal investigation. I wanted some fresh eyes in a place I considered to be haunted and therefore extremely active.

We carefully negotiated the steep stairs from Strachan Avenue down into the burial grounds. The group fanned out and started touring the perimeter as if they were old hands at investigative work. Almost right away they were taking photographs. Paul had brought a tape recorder and placed it on a wall that held a few remaining tombstones in place.

My wife Michelle and I headed east along the northern boundary, taking pictures along the way. We circled the eastern end and started west on the southern edge. Michelle took a picture of what might be described as an orb. I normally shy away from orb photos, as we take thousands of them, but this orb was the size of a full moon in the sky, and her second photo, taken just a moment later, showed nothing in the same location. Amanda joined us as we stood examining the photo.

We skirted a large puddle as Helen cut across the field to meet up with us. As she approached, Michelle snapped a photo of her, and there in the flash from the camera was the image of a man walking near her. Unfortunately, the image did not show up in the photograph. We continued down to the southwestern tree line, where most of the activity had been reported.

Paul moved along the memorial wall taking photos. He moved past the wall and along a short hedge, using his night vision scope to scan the darkness for movement. As he stood there, his keys, which were hanging from his belt, were pulled away from him and allowed to snap back against his leg. He spun around, but there was no one near him. He turned and doubled back to where part of the group was just past the flag post, but he heard the distinct footfalls of someone walking in the gravel behind him. He quickened his pace.

We started to break into smaller groups; some continued walking the cemetery while a few set out lawn chairs to sat quietly in the dark and observe. Amanda and I decided to head out for some hot drinks, since the air was growing chilly.

When we returned, everyone moved to the central area near the memorial wall. As we sat talking, Michelle heard a sound behind us, so she got up, noticing that Amanda had heard something as well. They moved together past the opening in the wall to investigate, but saw nothing. Michelle raised her camera and snapped a quick shot. Amanda again saw a man in the light of the flash. As Michelle took the photo, her camera, and Amanda's camera and cell phone, immediately shut off. They scanned the open field and saw nothing there. When they rejoined the team, Michelle turned her camera back on and searched for the photo she had just taken. There in the field was an odd grey mist that could not be explained.

Time was passing quickly. The place seemed very active, and everyone seemed excited about being there. Jonathan and Sarah set up their lawn chairs, and as they sat watching, they started to talk about ghosts and life after death. Jonathan described some experiences from his teenage years, and Sarah mentioned that she had never had an experience. Just as she said this, she clearly heard a man clear his throat directly behind her. Startled, she spun around but found no one there. Sarah and Jonathan decided to walk the northern tree line.

Amanda moved next to the memorial wall and was looking at the recovered grave markers when she felt something close to her. Her eyes started to water and she smelled cigar smoke.

Sarah, Jonathan, and Michelle moved along the tree line, splitting up to take individual positions in the shape of a triangle. As they investigated and photographed their respective areas, Michelle's eyes started to water. She could hear leaves rustling and twigs snapping as if someone was walking near her. Jonathan called her over, since he had seen a shadow that moved among the trees then vanished. Sarah motioned to Michelle and Jonathan to come right away. She was hearing branches snapping in the tree line just in front of her. The pair rushed over and moved into the trees, but nothing out of the ordinary was found.

Amanda arrived and told everyone that when at the bridge near the tree line, she could hear someone walking, but no one was there.

It was now late, and we were preparing to leave when I noticed a dark figure roaming the eastern section of the grounds. I looked through the night vision scope to get a better look. I put the scope to my eye and looked down the field but was unable to locate the person. I pulled the scope away and there he was, still milling about. I kept my eye on him and handed the scope to Sarah. She could also see him until she used the scope. Paul came over and tried, without any better luck. By this time the figure had vanished.

Courtesy Michelle Palmisano

Although it wasn't seen at the time, this glowing fog was captured moving amongst the trees in the cemetery.

We talked for a few more minutes then gathered our chairs and equipment and headed back towards Strachan Avenue.

The team pushed on, but Michelle and I hung back, talking. As we passed the larger, more mature trees in the middle of the cemetery, Michelle stopped and her eyes started to water. It has been observed that in many encounters with spirit energy, people's eyes will start to water for no reason. She turned to look back along the path, but nothing was there. We took a few photos then kept moving.

The next day Paul called me. Astoundingly, we had captured two EVPs. One was rough because of a slight wind, but it was a male voice calling for someone, sounding like "Pa."

The other was extremely clear: that of a male voice saying, "Yes, sir!"

Research on Stanley Barracks

This spirit at Stanley Barracks played on my mind. He had challenged us to catch him, which I interpreted as a challenge to find out who he was. If I could accomplish that, then maybe I could confront him and lessen his grip on Annie and the others there. In past investigations, I had found that some malevolent spirits are like comic book super-villains — find out their true identity, take away their anonymity, and you take away their power. That was exactly what I had in mind. Besides, he had physically attacked a member of my team, so in all fairness he was the one who had made it personal.

I knew from the way he conducted himself that he wasn't a soldier. The fact that he had a relationship with Annie and other females there was another clue. Michele had said the time frame was 1953, give or take a few years. Annie herself had given his first name as Bob, then the other females had given us the initial of his last name in the powder, the letter *M*.

I felt he was either a squatter or was housed at the barracks after the Second World War, either one of the unemployed or a welfare recipient. I knew he was bad-tempered and foulmouthed. He wasn't shy and he was most definitely a coward.

It took weeks of research, but I believed I had found Bob's full name.

The Barracks was used as emergency shelter from 1947 until the early part of the 1950s. In 1953, all but the officer's quarters were torn down.

I came across a newspaper article from August 1947 that described the horrible living conditions at the Barracks when had 150 families with 600 children lived there. A spokesman had come forward to speak for the families. He met on the property with then-mayor Saunders and complained about the dirt, filth, and horrible living conditions, including the bathrooms. He went on to say that living on the grounds of Exhibition Place while visitors swarmed all around was horrible, and those living there felt trapped.

To compound the deplorable situation within the Barracks, there were sporadic outbreaks of polio, and specific buildings were quarantined for weeks.

I read the article a few times, but my intuition told me that this spokesman was the guy. Was I right? I would need to go back to the barracks and talk to Bob.

Seventeenth Investigation

Stanley Barracks
September 2010

Paul, Amanda, Darrin, Michele, Sheryl, Jim, Anna, Linda, Christina, and Me

Paul, Amanda, Sheryl, and I arrived early to set up the surveillance equipment, and as promised, Linda and Christina were waiting. Security opened the southwest door, and we hauled the equipment in. The first system was set up on the first floor at the east end facing into the classroom. The second system was placed downstairs directly below the first, watching the hallway near the bathrooms. We placed a final camera in a large room in the basement next to a fireplace, looking west so that it could watch the entrance to the room and the servant door from the kitchen. As the instruments recorded, we went outside to wait for the rest of the team to arrive.

The surveillance equipment immediately started to capture activity. On the main floor there was whistling in the hallway and banging sounds, as if someone was working on repairs. There were heavy steps on the hardwood floors, the sound of boots, then a little girl giggling.

Outside, the sky was grey and threatening. Darrin, Michele, Jim, and Anna arrived, along with the rain. We all quickly went inside the Barracks and prepared our digital cameras, parabolic microphone, and portable digital recorders. I asked Michele to take the lead. She started up the stairs with the team following. She said she saw a woman running up the stairs ahead of us, all the way to the top floor. Although we had the urge to follow, we decided to do a room-to-room search, starting on the first floor.

We started at the west end, checking each room. Meanwhile, at the other end of the hall, the surveillance captured what sounded like an old-type phonograph that has to be wound up. Music started to play then stopped, then started again. Children giggled, and there was unintelligible gibberish. All activity came to an end with the EVP of a man saying "Jenny." All was quiet when the team worked closer to the room with the camera.

Fifty minutes in, I noticed a problem: the batteries in my camera were draining at an incredible rate. Normally I can take about seventy photos on the two batteries, but that evening I'd had to replace them five times, and I'd only taken forty photos. Darrin later told me that his digital movie camera and cell phone batteries seemed to be draining extremely fast, and some of the other team members were having similar problems. In past investigations, this phenomenon had usually indicated that something was about to happen. What that might be was anyone's guess.

Michele stopped in the doorway of the room across the hall from the one with our camera. "There are four men here. They seem to be oblivious to us. One is wearing a ball cap, two have glasses on, and the fourth is wearing a dirty T-shirt."

Sheryl, Darrin, and I stepped into the room, and although we saw nothing out of the ordinary, we did notice it was noticeably colder than the rest of the building. Sheryl moved into the centre of the room, and Michele said the men dispersed like they were mist. She found it hard to believe that we hadn't seen them.

She then led us into the classroom. "I hear so much noise in here, like there are fifty people all talking at once." She moved towards the back door, to another small hallway, and almost stumbled. "I just saw a cat, where did it go?" she asked, looking around. "It was brown and grey!"

It was interesting to note that this was the room where on previous visits we had captured EVPs of a cat meowing.

"There is no cat," I reported.

We went out into the main hall and Michele stopped.

"Let's go upstairs," I said, pointing to the stairway.

"That's where I saw that woman go up."

As we left, the first floor camera recorded wooden wheels rolling on the hardwood and sigh and a bang as if someone had put something heavy down. Then a male voice called "Jenny," followed by a few more bangs, then the sound of tinkling glass.

"There is an Elizabeth here, I just heard someone call her. An older male passed in this room. I don't feel well in here. He had stomach problems, missing part of his leg, S initial, grey hair. Major pain in my head, like I should just drop. I keep hearing about letters going home, that they are important."

Amanda felt dizzy, like there was fast-paced energy, a lot of movement.

"Oh, there is a lot of energy here, men running, yelling and screaming, the hall is filling with people," Michele said.

We moved into another room. "It's nice in here, quiet. I feel a bit drunk and I hear music." Sheryl and I both smelled the sweet scent of pipe smoke just as Michele said, "I smell pipe smoke in here. Wow, there are a lot of children around. Keep a watch for little hands pulling on your clothing."

On the main floor the system recorded heavy footsteps and a male voice calling "Jenny, Jenny."

We entered a room that had been previously off limits to us. We entered and I stopped short: an extremely long and narrow set of folding stairs to an attic stretched out ahead of us.

"This is new. Can I go up?" Michele asked.

"Be careful," I said, looking up the length of the stairs.

Michele and Sheryl climbed first, leading with their flashlights. Immediately Sheryl felt surrounded by people. "The atmosphere is horrible. It's sickening up here," she said as she backed down the steps.

Michele snapped two photos and followed her down to the floor below. "Not nice up there. It's loaded with people, all around, horrible," she told us.

Paul and I moved up the stairs, and Paul used his night vision scope to investigate the massive space. I was standing on the stairs just below him as I felt my hair being played with. I quickly turned and switched on my flashlight to examine the area, looking for a cobweb that might have caught my hair. I discovered nothing to explain what I had felt.

"Crap, there's a large black mass moving in the far corner of the room!" Paul said.

I moved up higher on the steps, and he handed me the scope. I scanned the area but saw nothing … until it moved. It was a massive, black, misty shadow that I could barely see through the wooden support beams. It seemed to fold itself into the corner, where it vanished. I handed back the scope and took several photos of the area, then we climbed down.

Sheryl felt something unseen hanging off her left shoulder. She didn't feel well. Michele came over to her and said, "Someone is hanging on to you." She worked to free Sheryl of the energy.

Anna felt a presence move directly behind her, watching her intently, so she moved away and joined the others.

Michele looked around and started counting people in the room, but each time she counted she ended up with three more than there should have been. Anna paled as Michele pointed to where she was standing and said, "Those three are right there."

We left the area and stopped in the last room on the floor. I could see that some of the team members were slightly shaken by what happened in the attic, and I knew we should take a break, but we also needed to finish this floor.

"There is a child in here, playing hide and go seek. I get the name James. He was hung here, either a lynching or suicide. A horrible feeling."

The digital recorder captured a cat meowing.

As the team moved out into the rain and fresher air for a break, Jim, Paul, and I checked the equipment. We changed the DVDs in the basement. As we changed the one on the first floor and were walking back to the exit, we stopped as something just ahead of us started to walk away. We heard the footsteps on the floor as the boards creaked, but we could not see what was causing the sounds. I have to admit it felt better outside in the rain.

When we went back in, we prepared to move down into the basement.

"'They're coming,' is what I am hearing," Michele told us as we checked our portable equipment.

She took the lead with Amanda directly behind her. As they pushed through the doors to the basement, they stopped. They looked at each other; both had heard an audible growl.

Courtesy Michelle Palmisano

Paul and Amanda investigate a strange sound at Stanley Barracks.

Michele raised her eyebrows. "Huh," was all she could muster.

They stepped through the doors and stopped again. "There is so much negative energy down here!" Michele headed directly to the women's washroom. As she turned to enter, she gasped and jumped back, startled. "David was right here. He put his face right in front of me."

Paul told David off and antagonized him.

"There are other people coming in, Jack. They're not sorry," Michele told us.

There were noises in the hall, and Paul went to investigate. "They're gone, they left with Paul," Michele said.

She led the team back into the hallway and down to the men's bathroom. "They keep calling Paul the 'little man.'"

"Oh, they have been in your car. Do you have a bag behind your driver's seat?" Michele asked Paul.

"Yes," he replied.

"Just be aware, they have been around you."

Paul was not pleased.

The team started down the stairs to the basement. Darrin lagged behind as his movie camera started to malfunction. The MiniDV had stopped and would not record. It seemed to have not only failed, but was jammed. He ejected the MiniDV and replaced it with another, but the same problem occurred. He replaced it again with no luck.

Led by Michele, the team entered the women's washroom and fanned out into the room.

Outside in the hall, the surveillance system captured EVPs of a male voice calling out, "Annie ... Annie ... Annie," and "Damn it ... damn it."

The camera moved slightly, all went quiet, then the whispers started.

"I feel sad in here, like I could just cry. Emotionally drained. Very depressed," Michele said.

An EVP whisper from a female voice said "Sad."

Both cameras in the basement stopped recording.

"I hear Cathy, or Katherine, over and over again. Major pressure, fighting, arguing, two men arguing, there is bloodshed, Patrick, lots of drinking, tough guy. Annie, B ... B ... Bob, David, help."

An EVP was recorded of a male voice speaking in an unknown language.

Anna started to feel overwhelming emotion, so she moved closer to Jim, who was experiencing a heavy feeling in his chest that was making it hard to breathe. Anna closed her eyes as she became light-headed, as though she might be sick and losing her balance. Jim helped her stay on her feet.

Michele was now murmuring, eyes closed, swaying. Amanda was sitting in a chair and jumped up and moved to her side to steady her. "Are you okay?" she asked, but Michele gave no reply. "Are you okay?" Amanda asked again. Michele turned to her, looking blank, then completely broke down. Paul stepped in and took Michele out of the bathroom, into the hall, and rushed her towards the exit past Darrin, whose camera then started to work. The team followed.

Both cameras in the basement had inexplicably started to record again.

Through her tears, Michele said, "I just went through the whole thing. Oh my God. That poor girl; the screaming, being dragged and raped by those two men, Bob and David. Oh my God, the energy in that room."

Paul helped Michele light a cigarette, hands shaking.

"The beating, rape. Oh my God, they kicked her repeatedly … He knew, he knew I wasn't prepared for that. I felt her come into the room and then I was her." She broke down again. "I feel like I'm going to be sick." She was trembling. "Most horrible thing ever. She was screaming so loud, and no one came. Stop Bob, stop David. Why did they cut off her baby finger? That poor, poor girl."

There was no one in the basement, but the cameras recorded activity.

An EVP of male voice said, "Annie." The men's washroom stall door slammed. The male voice called "Annie" again, then the camera moved slightly from left to right.

The system recorded footsteps, then shuffling, but nothing was visible. Then there was a clanging sound as if someone was banging two pipes together. The washroom stall door slammed again. All went quiet.

We give Michele some time to recover, then she decided that she wanted to continue the investigation.

We went back down to the basement. Anna walked down the hall under view of the surveillance camera. A female voice called out "Hey." Amanda followed behind her and again the voice said "Hey."

An EVP of a male voice is recorded saying, "Annie … Annie."

An EVP from the system near the men's bathroom recorded the voice of a female saying, "Take that!"

"I'm getting a heavy head again," Michelle said as we all moved into the women's bathroom.

"Is there anyone here? Can you give us a sign? You let me see before … Oh!" Michelle jumped back. "Oh, right up in my face … don't do that."

"What was it?" Paul asked.

"David. His face popped up right in front of mine. Give me a sign you are here … he's here. David."

An EVP was captured of a male voice calling "David … Annie."

"David, why don't you push me? Such a big man. Where is your buddy Bob? Why don't you both come in here? You guys are just punks picking on women," Paul said, moving deeper into the bathroom.

An EVP of a male voice said, "David."

"There are others coming in now … Jack. Those two are not sorry," Michele said.

"You said that before. What does this mean?" I asked her.

"Jack knows what they did. He caught them but they don't care. Jack never said anything, he let it go," Michele explained.

A bell tolled on the digital recorder, but it was not heard at the time.

Paul walked out into the hall and over to the large room with the fireplace. An EVP recorded a male voice: "Hey, Annie."

"Watch out, here I come!" Michele blurted out. "There're gone, they left with Paul."

There was an unknown language captured on the digital recorder again that sounded like Mandarin. Paul came back into the bathroom.

"They are after you," Michele told him.

An EVP of male voice said, "Yeah."

"They are after me," Paul said, laughing. "Let them come. Hey, Bobby, come and get me!"

An EVP of male voice said, "Get me … get me."

"They call you little man," Michele said.

She moved down the hall to the men's washroom, knocking on the wall. "Anyone here? Give us a sign. Make a noise, do something." She looked at Paul. "They have it bad for you right now. Oh my God."

"Well, come out, fellas! I'm waiting for you, come get me," Paul taunted them again.

"They are showing me your car again, the back seat."

"Hmm," Paul replied.

"They show me this to let you know they have been in your car with you. David's a little bit more brazen, Bob hides in the shadows. He doesn't like to come out. Now they are gone … nothing."

We waited a few minutes then headed back to the women's washroom. As we entered, the atmosphere was heavy and thick, almost sickening.

"Oh, it's bad in here," Paul said. "Annie, are you here?"

An EVP of female voice said, "Yes."

"She is here," Michele said.

"We won't let them hurt you anymore," Paul said.

"She says you can't stop them."

"Give us a sign you are here."

Sheryl grabbed her knee in pain. "I just got kicked in the knee."

"Cowards! Hit me, Bob," Paul demanded.

"Picking on the girls," Michele added. "It's gone quiet. Come on, Annie, who kicked Sheryl? Can you give us a name? Nothing, it's gone completely quiet."

We stopped for a break.

I knew I had a great team, but how much more of this would they take? It was horrible enough being around these two foul spirits, but to have my team members assaulted was too much. I started considering pulling out of the Barracks.

The camera in the hall moved ever so slightly.

THE EXPERIMENT

I had planned an experiment for the right location, and my criteria were simple: it had to be haunted and it had to be fairly active. I felt the basement of the Barracks fit both requirements perfectly.

Almost ten years earlier I had formulated a theory about what a ghost was and where it might dwell. I believed the secret was a natural divider that separated our reality from theirs, and that divider is frequency. At the time I was working very closely with people who were up to speed on science and technology and who understood what I was trying to do. After a great deal of speculation, planning, and field experiments to gather further data, we finally devised a way to attempt to synchronize both realities. If this worked, it would be a major breakthrough in parapsychology, but it was also a terrifying prospect, since what I was about to try would transcend a boundary no one had crossed before. No one knew what the impact or consequences would be.

The first field trial was set up in haunted servant quarters at a location I was investigating during the *Overshadows* project. I knew it was extremely haunted and very active. This seemed the best place for the first test.

All the equipment was assembled, and two team members and a self proclaimed skeptic were invited to attend. The equipment was turned on, producing a low, thumping sound. I knew the system was building a standing wave within the frequency I had selected. We waited.

What occurred a short time later changed the way I thought about spirits and the afterlife.

Everyone started to experience auditory phenomena, the floors began to creak, and we heard hollow sounds of walking and whispers from all directions. The room started to turn hot and the air changed, as if black soot was floating on the air. Black shadows started to move out of nowhere, and the shadows turned into the shapes of people skirting along the walls. Panic erupted in the room. I wasn't sure who was first, but my skeptic friend was the first to flee the house. Someone shut off the equipment, and the room returned to normal.

Did we just get a look into another reality? It was unfortunate that the experiment was cut short, as I felt confident that we were about to come face-to-face with the deceased. I couldn't even begin to contemplate what that we could have accomplished had we had run the experiment for just two more minutes.

The second time I ran the experiment was at the Fusion house in Mississauga. Although I had tested and re-checked the equipment several times before arriving at the house and had one of my best technical people with me, the simplest yet most important components failed when we set them up. A simple LED on the frequency generator would not operate. This small thing made the experiment impossible, since I could not set the required frequency and would not be able to tell exactly what I was doing. As most of the team mused, it seemed like a higher power had intervened, and the statement was a loud and clear "No."

Tonight I was hoping we would have the opportunity for results.

As we headed back down to the basement, a male voice called for "Jenny."

We set up the equipment in the large room in the basement with the fireplace. The team filed in.

I set the frequency and turned on the speakers.

Michele began, "Annie, are you here?"

An EVP of a female voice said, "Yes."

The digital recorder captured an EVP of a male with a European accent saying "Oh my God."

Michele continued, "Bob, David."

Although the frequency was locked on the generator, it started to cycle down without explanation.

"It's really cold," Paul said.

An EVP of male voice agreed, "Yeah."

Paul walked over to Michele. She stepped back, looking at him. "You brought the cold with you. They are telling me they are near you."

Paul walked across the room towards me, and when he was about three feet from me, I felt the temperature drop fast. As he arrived next to me, it felt as though I was standing in a freezer. Whatever was surrounding him was pushing the air temperature down by twenty-one degrees.

I noticed that the system was somehow cycling down to even lower frequencies. It now seemed like my equipment had been hijacked and was out of my control. Without a plan for dealing with that, I switched off the system.

"Has this ever happened before?" Darrin asked.

"No, never."

After a brief discussion, we decided to try the experiment in the women's washroom. We hauled the equipment across the hall. Darrin was the last one out of the big room, and an EVP captured a male voice saying, "Psssst."

After moving the equipment, we reconvened in the women's bathroom. I switched on the equipment and set the frequency, locking the dial.

"Annie, we want to talk to you," Michele started.

There was a female response that Michele, Sheryl, and Amanda all heard. The system recorded a female EVP saying, "Yes."

Michele looked at Paul as if asking him to go stand somewhere else. "You still have that cold around you."

"I know." Paul moved to the door.

The digital recorder captured a male voice. "John, John."

"John is now here," Michele said.

Although the digital recorder captured a male talking, the words were unintelligible.

"I hear you talking. I just can't hear what you are saying," Michele said. "If you have something to say, say it loud so we can hear."

Anna and Jim were feeling uneasy.

"Annie is here."

Darrin was overwhelmed by emotions: he felt fear, panic, shame, and then anger. He tried to push the feelings away, as he knew none of these were his.

"I feel your sadness," Michele said.

Darrin's camera light started to blink.

"They are here, Bob and Dave."

The camera moved slightly, and the sound cut in and out.

"What do you want us to know? You had a child. Keep the light on please. Don't let them turn off the light. She runs through this building to get away from them. She had a child by one of them and the child died."

An EVP of a male voice said, "Damn it." Another male EVP said, "Get out."

Darrin started to feel odd emotions again, this time of happiness and pleasure, but they were twisted. They were derived from doing negative things to other people. He was on the verge of being sick to his stomach.

"Bob is near Darrin, playing with the light. Step away from him, Bob! Jason is here, I don't know who Jason is."

The light started blinking faster. Then it stopped blinking.

"They are gone," Michele reported.

We waited a few minutes, but nothing further happened. Michele shrugged.

I stepped in and shut the equipment down. It was late and our time was up.

I was disappointed with the results. The experiment in the large room seemed to work well at first, but then the frequency selector switch had started moving on its own. The experiment is designed to work within very specific parameters, and I felt something was hijacking the project. The bathroom portion was something of a failure, since the equipment was designed for the large size of the fireplace room, not a small bathroom. This would have distorted the standing wave, changing it from my original calculations.

Courtesy Paul Palmisano

Paul captured an image of Bob on the door next to the bathrooms. Under close examination he is older, late forties or early fifties, with thick a moustache and a high forehead.

There wasn't much I could do. Some of these things go way beyond my control, and other inherent problems come with trying to do major work on a poor man's budget.

Eighteenth Investigation

Fire Hall, Scadding Cabin, and Fort Rouillé
October 2010

Paul, Jim, Anna, Linda, Christina, and Me

We arrived at the Fire Hall and were given access via the rear door by a police officer working at the station next door.

The rear door opened into a large kitchen and dining area, with a bathroom and office to the left. The main floor was a large, open area for fire vehicles to park in, with a centre staircase dividing the space. Upstairs was an open floor normally filled with beds. At the other end of the floor opposite the stairs was the fire pole.

We set up one camera on the second floor facing the stairs and pole, and the second was placed on the main floor looking across the empty parking bay to the stairs and kitchen door. The systems were now active and recording, so we left the building and proceeded to our next location.

The oldest building on the property is Scadding Cabin, built in 1794 for John Scadding, who had accompanied Lieutenant Governor John Graves Simcoe to Upper Canada. In 1879, the cabin was moved by the York Pioneer Historical Society from the east bank of the Don River to its present location.

We drove to the cabin and parked looking over the grounds where the ancient structure sits. Not far away is the patch of land where Fort Rouillé once stood.

Linda unlocked the door for us. Paul set an audio recording system on the stairs leading to a small bedroom on the second storey. I placed a

Courtesy Exhibition Place Archives

The Fire Hall was built in 1912 by George W. Gouinlock. His design was Tudor Revival and was used by emergency services during the Exhibition.

handheld digital flash recorder on the fireplace mantle facing the stairs. Again the systems were set to record, and we moved outside and locked the door.

Also known as Fort Toronto, Fort Rouillé was established by the French around 1749 as a trading post. In July 1759, as British troops advanced, the French, feeling the fort could not be defended, decided to burn it down to prevent the British from using it. The French then retreated to Montreal.

Several bodies have been unearthed at that fortification and identified by their uniform buttons. They more than likely died from disease or from the harsh winters.

We walked the grounds and stopped at the site of Fort Rouillé, reading the historic plaques and inspecting the cannons. Although the fort was French, the cannons presently there are British. After some time

Courtesy Exhibition Place Archives

Scadding Cabin, 1934

passed, we noticed the only things patrolling the perimeter of the old fort's boundaries were two well-fed raccoons.

Our time was up and we backtracked, collecting our equipment. Paul took it home for analysis.

SURVEILLANCE RESULTS

The upper floor system at the Fire Hall captured a loud bang and a male talking, but the message was unintelligible.

The lower floor system captured banging, the sound of something like metal being dropped, then a clear EVP of what sounded like an older male saying "Get out ... this fire house!"

It seemed that there was something there. It made sense, simply because of the building's age, that sometime in its long history someone would have developed an attachment to this structure.

In Scadding Cabin, both systems, being in close proximity, recorded the same things: a loud bang as if someone had slammed their hand down on a table, then a female sobbing.

It was a sad sound, but we were not getting any more information. Maybe if we'd continued the investigation, we could have come closer to finding out who this woman was, or why she seemed so sad.

Nineteenth Investigation

Stanley Barracks
October 2010

Paul, Amanda J., Sheryl, Alex, Amanda K., Peter, Christina, and Me

The team arrived early, since I wanted to get in and set up surveillance before the medium arrived. Tonight we were going to try a new medium Alex had introduced me to. Alex and Amanda Keays would arrive later this evening. It was my mission to get into the newly discovered attic and see what we might find there.

We entered through the southwest door. The building was extremely hot, and we dropped our coats on the main floor. Paul, Peter, and I set up the surveillance systems right away, placing a camera on the first floor, midway looking east, another in the large room at the east end of the building on the main floor, and a final system on the second floor.

Amanda J. sensed a rushing or fast-paced energy that made her feel sick.

We discovered that although we had specifically come to the Barracks to take an in-depth look at the newly discovered attic, we were disappointed to find someone had sealed the retractable stairs.

Once the systems were recording, we went outside to wait for Alex and Amanda K. to arrive.

Inside, the cameras started to capture activity. A wooden door closed not far from the first floor camera, and there were heavy footsteps on the floor. A male called for Jenny, and a thin black image streaked across the camera's view from the adjoining hall to the classroom, vanishing

In this window there seems to be the image of an Aboriginal man in the left middle portion, and in the middle panel to the right is a strange image of a deer.

through the stairway door across the hall. The male called to Jenny again and heavy banging started coming from every direction.

Paul and I speculated about the tugboat just west of Stanley Barracks. Could it be haunted and, more importantly, could we get access to it? It was named the *Ned Hanlan* after Edward Ned Hanlan (1855–1908), who was a world champion sculler and the namesake for Hanlan's Point on Toronto Island. This was the boat Prime Minister John Diefenbaker used to tour the coast of Lake Ontario, trying to convince Torontonians he still cared about them, even though he had just cancelled the Avro Arrow contracts and was shutting down the entire project. When the boat was eventually decommissioned and was about to be sold for scrap, several Progressive Conservatives saved it and had it shipped to Exhibition Place, thinking there might one day be a monument built to Diefenbaker. When Ned Hanlan's descendants said that Ned had been a Liberal and would never have supported Diefenbaker, the boat sat in limbo and has been deteriorating ever since.

Alex and Amanda K. arrived and parked near the Barracks. As we stood out front planning our strategy, a banging started. It was loud and violent and seemed to come from every direction. This would later be evident on all of our recording equipment.

We decided to conduct a walkthrough with Amanda K. in the lead. Starting on the top floor moving from west to east, we headed inside and up the stairs. All seemed quiet, although the earlier banging had unnerved some of us.

The camera captured an EVP of a male voice calling "Henry" on the main floor.

As we strolled the hall, Amanda K. stopped and entered a room on the south side. "I am coming in here because I saw a white shadow, a face … I'm picking up an Oliver." She crossed the room and sat in a chair by the window. She felt that there was a child present, the spirit of a little boy. She sat quietly for a few moments then asked if he wanted to communicate with us.

Collection of the author

Amanda Keays sits communicating with a little boy named Oliver, while Peter (left) and Amanda Jobe (right) look on. No one saw the strange energy rising above the medium.

Amanda J. was off to the right using the parabolic microphone. "I heard him say 'yes,'" she reported. The response was captured on the digital recorder.

"You heard him as well," Amanda K. said, smiling. "I see the child is here, but there is someone else. I don't know who they are. They are asking questions. They want to know what we're doing here. I'm being questioned. It's a male. I can't see who he is, they are blocking me, but I can see the little boy here. He has a cute mushroom-style haircut, he's about five years old, and he wants to play. He keeps coming over to touch my hand then leaves again. They are curious."

"What was his name?" Paul asked.

"Oliver."

"What year is it for Oliver?"

Amanda K. paused for a moment. "18 ... 1878."

Communication stopped and the team moved on.

On the first floor, at the east end of the hallway, an ominous, greyish-black object started to form on the floor, with no definable shape.

A male voice yelled, "Hey," then there was whispering back and forth as this shape grew larger.

A male called for "Henry" again then the shape faded away. As it vanished, the main floor camera started to crackle with static, and the image distorted as if pulled at odd angles by a large magnet. Through the static you can barely make out something moving near the camera.

Oliver, as drawn by Amanda Keays.

As we completed our tour of the second floor and headed to the stairwell, Paul photographed the window at the end of the hall, facing east.

Then came the sound of steel banging on steel. The camera on the first floor recorded footsteps then a male voice, saying "Get back."

The team moved along the first floor. Amanda K. said, "I have a feeling that poltergeist activity takes place here. Things move and items may be found missing, only to turn up in unlikely places. As I'm walking down these halls, I feel like I'm in jail. It's weird, like someone was held here against their will, like a prison. I feel like I just want to get out of here."

An EVP of a male voice said, "Hey, get back."

We entered a room that we called the classroom, where one of our surveillance cameras was recording.

"I see blood, a puddle of blood. Someone has tried to clean it up, to cover it up. It's creepy, but I keep hearing 'Don't tell anyone, no one needs to know.' There are lots of secrets here." Amanda K. crossed the room and stopped by a large table. "I'm picking up on a love affair, two people that aren't supposed to be together, also an older gentleman who is very negative … negative energy. Doesn't want us here. He is very rude and is yelling at me. He is tall and big, not fat but rather a solid man, with short grey hair. He is not happy at all, doesn't want me talking about things that have gone on here. He's swearing at me. Some things I've already said he is angry about."

Although we couldn't hear it, the camera in the room captured banging. An EVP of a male voice said, "Dave." There was an undecipherable muffled response. An EVP of a male voice said, "You bitch."

"He's yelling at me. 'Why are you here? Get the fuck out, who do you think you are?'" Amanda K. told us.

An EVP of a male voice said, "Get out."

"There is stuff you will find out that he doesn't want you to know," she said.

"All right. Let's step out of this room for now," I said.

We stepped outside for a break, and the cooler air was well-received.

There was no one in the building, but the surveillance systems continued to record activity. A male voice called "Henry" twice then the banging started again. As the sound trailed off, a man called "Jenny," and a little girl giggled.

The team re-entered the Barracks and headed directly down to the basement.

"I see fire, something about a fire," Amanda K. reported as we moved down the hallway.

We made it to the end of the hall and entered the men's washroom. Amanda K. moved to the far wall and paused in thought. "I am picking up on a fight between two men. They both have knives and are circling each other, trying to get at each other. It's over money, like a wager, and one doesn't want to pay up. Benjamin." She laughed. "It's not even a lot of money, such a small amount. There's a lot of gambling going on here."

We moved back into the hall. "There's actually the spirit of a cat here in the building," Amanda K. told us.

SIXTEEN STITCHES NEEDED FOR CUTS IN FIGHT

A 30-year-old needed 16 stitches to close head wounds received in a fight at Stanley Barracks Saturday night, police at Cowan Avenue station said today. They charged a 16-year-old resident of the Barracks with assault causing bodily harm.

Toronto Star, May 23, 1949

We entered the women's washroom. "They all roam. There is a woman standing in the doorway. She thinks it's funny that we're all in the bathroom. They're very curious about what we are doing here, because no one has communicated with them for such a long time. They are interested."

We crossed the hall and went into the large room with the fireplace.

"I see a little girl. I don't think she is a visitor. She's always here, because something really bad has happened to her. I keep getting images of her with her family, then she wanders off and something happens to her. Something catches her eye and she leaves, something happens with her neck. I'm not sure, tightness on my neck, I can't breathe."

Two floors above us, a male voice called for Dan, and something was heard running down the hallway.

"There are a lot of kids around, sickness, illness, going around ... I don't know. A man with an injury to his leg ... looks like he had his leg amputated, it's gone." She paused. "A bullet to the leg, infection, gangrene.

Could the little girl that Amanda Keays saw be Jenny?

He hasn't passed over, busy doing stuff. He's in his own little world. He has to do something for his commander. He's a courier, something important. I also sense head trauma."

On the upper floor the camera in the classroom recorded someone calling "Jenny." There were shuffling sounds near the camera and then something banged into the table, causing it to move slightly and the table leg to scrape on the wood floor. In the hall someone was whistling.

"I'm picking up on an older lady. She's a big, burly woman. Her dress goes to the floor and she wears an apron over her dress. Her hair is up tight and she's wearing a bonnet, like a frilly hat thing. Wears glasses. She looks like she's had a lot of sun. She works outside a lot, she's a working woman, not well-to-do or privileged, a servant of sorts. Her cheeks are rosy. She had an accent, Irish or British. She's loving and caring, like being a nanny and taking care of children. She remains here and watches over the place and people. She loves this place and is connected to it. If people come here and find a penny or a feather on the ground, it would be from her, letting you know she is still here. One time, she may have even scared away people who tried to break in here. I get a very protective feeling from her. This place holds a very special place in her heart. She may have come over here with a family, but she didn't have children of her own. But I see kids around her. She knows there are people here. There is a lady who comes here to work to whom she has a connection, and sometimes ghosts will form a special bond with the living."

Courtesy Peter Roe

ABOVE: As Peter was about to leave, he snapped a few parting photos of the south face of the Barracks. He later discovered a man looking out the window, watching us depart.

RIGHT: A drawing by Amanda Keays showing what the friendly woman looked like.

I stepped out into the hall and spoke with Christina, who told me that there was a woman working here. It was interesting to note that on a previous visit a window, was open, which we couldn't explain, and that particular window belonged to the office of the woman who worked there.

I would have loved to stay longer, since the old place seemed active, but our time had run out. The team moved to the main floor to collect their jackets as Paul, Peter, and I headed off to gather the equipment.

As we walked towards the classroom and passed the camera in the hall, it recorded whispers of a male voice yelling, "Get out."

We packed up and left the building. I thanked Amanda K. and Alex for coming out, and everyone headed off.

As I started the car, Amanda J. looked up and briefly saw the image of a cat in the first floor window. By the time I looked up, it was gone.

Twentieth Investigation

Stanley Barracks, Scadding Cabin, and the Bandshell
October 2010

Paul, Michelle, Sarah, Peter, Jim, Anna,
Linda, Christina, Nathan, and Me

The team assembled at the General Services Building, where we met Christina and Nathan. The night was overcast and raining, there was a lot of vehicle traffic on the grounds. We left most of our cars in the General Services parking area, and the rest followed my vehicle over to Scadding Cabin. Paul set up two recording systems, one on the main floor and the second in the tiny bedroom in the loft. We had a quick look around the area and then we piled into the vehicles and drove to the bandshell.

Peter was the first out of the car. He took photos as the rest of us waited for security to arrive and open the door. We talked about the history of the building and all the fascinating performances that have taken place there. Security pulled up and provided us with access.

After a quick tour, we placed a surveillance camera in a long hallway on the lower level. After taking a number of photographs, we headed over to the Barracks.

Linda had been kind enough to secure access to the attic and had maintenance staff leave it open for the evening. This was very exciting, considering what we'd felt and seen the first time we entered the space.

As we filed into the building, we were pleased to find that it wasn't as hot as on our last visit. We placed a camera in the basement, midway down the hall facing east towards the bathrooms. Another camera was set up on the first floor, mid-hallway, looking east towards the classroom.

Courtesy Exhibition Place Archives

This Art Deco building was inspired by the Hollywood Bowl and was built in 1936.

The team split up. We swept the area with hand-held digital recorders and took photographs.

Sarah and my wife Michelle had been asked to come tonight to target specific locations within the barracks, places where photos had shown anomalies on the last visit. They would find those places and shoot pictures from exact positions in a variety of ways to see if they could recreate what was captured the first time.

Several of us moved up to the attic, climbing the narrow stairs single file, pushing up into the cavernous pitch-black expanse. We started taking photos immediately.

When Nathan found a light switch, and the attic glowed with overhead lighting, several of us even cheered.

In the basement the camera captured the EVP of a male voice calling "Annie." There was a female response: "Yeah." Then the camera system shut off.

Collection of the author

As Sarah and Jim explored the attic of Stanley Barracks, Peter captured a photo of a column of energy, just slightly left of centre. Could this be the column Paul, Amanda, and I saw on the second floor?

After a good tour of the attic area, I set up a mini camera about fifteen feet from the stairs and placed a plasma disc in the foreground. A plasma disc is sound and motion activated. Any activity near the disk would cause blue lightning to flash across its face. Once everything was set, everyone went down to the lower floors to continue our investigation.

Paul, Jim, Anna, and Linda moved into a room and inspected fingerprints left in the dust on a fireplace mantle. Paul confirmed that the prints were fresh, but no one had been in the building since our last visit. Anna heard whispering, and as they moved into the hall they all heard a female humming.

Anna called out "Hello," and all went quiet, or so they thought. The camera recorded whispering and a male who called "David" twice.

Peter came up from the basement and told me that the surveillance system was off. I gathered Paul and Jim, and we headed down with Peter to the basement to find out what had happened to the camera system. After close examination, we discovered it had nothing to do with paranormal activity, but rather the electrical plug receptacle had failed. We found a new plug and reset the system.

Paul pointed out a faint female humming in the distance, coming from the fireplace room at the end of the hall. We all listened, and we could just hear her.

The team filtered up through the building, and we ended up on the second floor. Sarah and Michelle examined the room where Amanda K. had made contact with Oliver.

On the main floor, the camera in the hall recorded a male calling "Jenny," then a stern warning of, "Get back … now."

A male EVP said, "Henry."

Another male EVP, sounding annoyed, said, "What."

There was a great deal of whispering and a loud bang, then the sounds of things moving around. The banging started close to the camera, which was then replaced by a light tapping sound very close to our system.

In the background the camera microphone detected us coming down the stairs.

A male EVP said, "Get back."

As we entered the first floor from the east stairs, there was a male EVP saying, "Get out … now."

Everyone arrived at the southwest stairs for a break, and I headed out with Michelle and Sarah to pick up coffee. Paul, Anna, and Jim wandered down the first floor hallway, exploring the rooms along the way. They all heard a man yell "Hello," so they headed back to the rest of the team, thinking I had returned with the drinks. They all stated that the voice sounded exactly like mine, but I had not yet returned.

Ten minutes later we got back with the coffee, and they told me what had happened. As we stood talking near the exit, the camera on the main floor was still recording. It was interesting to hear the recording later, not because it contained anything earth-shattering, but because it was funny. The system had recorded us huddled in a group talking and making strategy plans, but it also recorded a group whispering at the other end of the hall. It was as though we were opposing football teams preparing our next play.

After we finished our drinks, everyone split up into smaller teams and we spread throughout the building. The first floor camera captured EVPs: "Henry."

"What?"

"Henry."

"What now?"

The team filtered up to the second floor. There came a sound from the stairway that some described as a moan and others as a female cry. This seemed to put most on edge, since the activity was becoming more physical.

Paul, Jim, Anna, and Peter headed back down to the first floor. Paul heard a male say "Hey" on the stairs, which made him stop, but he couldn't see anything.

They moved down the first floor hall and ended up in a small theatre room. As they sat listening quietly, they heard two sharp whistles in the hall. Paul stepped out of the room and yelled, "Who's down there?" But there was no one else on the floor.

Paul and Peter walked down to see if they could find the source of the sound while Jim and Anna stayed in the room.

"Bob, are you here?" Anna asked.

She pulled back defensively as she felt something touch her breast. Jim's eyes widened as he quite clearly noticed greyish dusty fingerprints on the front of her black sweater. They left the room quickly and caught up with Paul and Peter.

In the basement the camera was recording activity.

"Annie."

Big bang.

"Annie, Annie."

Shuffling sounds.

"David."

"Damn it."

Whispering.

We continued to examine the attic. Our time was running out, and everyone was excited at what was happening, but we still had to go to the other sites to collect our equipment.

Paul went down to the second floor to take a few more photos. His attention was caught by a muffled conversation in the split stairway at the far west end of the building. He could tell it was between two different men and a woman, but he could not hear what was being said. He moved slowly closer to the stairs and peered down. No one was there, and the sounds abruptly stopped.

We packed up and prepared to head out. I quietly said goodbye to the unseen inhabitants, thanking them for allowing me to visit.

We headed over to the bandshell and started tearing down the system there. Paul, Peter, Jim, Christina, and Anna walked over to Scadding Cabin to pick up the recording systems there. As they approached the cabin, something came out of the night at them, and Peter took a photo.

It looked like a large mist, so he took several control photos in which nothing showed up.

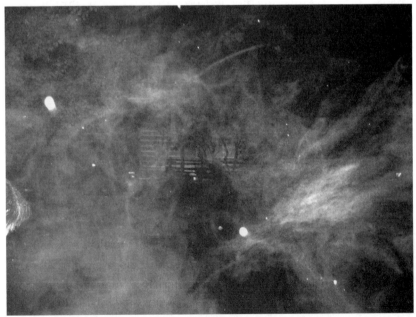

This mist was seen coming out of the woods near Scadding Cabin.

They reached the cabin and retrieved the equipment. On the way out Peter started to snap more photos. All were clear until he got to almost the same place as before, where his camera again caught the strange mist.

They made their way back and we all said goodnight.

Paul called me a few days later with the surveillance results.

Although the Barracks were extremely active, the bandshell hadn't produced a sound. I found this funny, since we had detected music in some of the most unlikely places, including the General Services Building stairwell and within Stanley Barracks. But in that remarkable building, all remained silent. Even though we had recorded a woman on a previous visit to Scadding Cabin, this time there was nothing at all on the recordings.

Twenty-First Investigation

General Services Building
November 2010

Paul, Peter, Michele, Amanda K., Amanda J., Darrin, Alex, Linda, Christina, and Me

We were going back to where we had started the investigation thirteen months earlier — the General Services Building. I suppose we had now come full circle in our work there. The stories of ghostly activity continued to seep out of this building on a weekly basis from security and other workers. It was still unclear why this building housed so many different spirits with seemingly no tie to its past, although there was a great deal of speculation. The best theory was that the power generation system and high voltage towers drew them to this place like a magnet, but we just didn't know for sure.

I was going to do something this night that I rarely do: I would bring two mediums and allow them to work alongside each other. I don't normally do this, but due to the fact that this was our last night there, I wanted to try combining their energy and see what might happen.

We met with Christina and moved to the third floor, where Paul and I set up a camera in the long main hallway at the far north end looking south. As we were placing the other camera in the archive, near the kitchenette facing the stacks, a banging started up. Paul gave me a pained look. "What the heck is that? Is that normal?"

"No, not really. Maybe it's the heating system," I said.

"Well, if it keeps up, we won't be getting many EVPs in here."

Once everything was set up and recording, we went to the office to wait for Michele and Darrin to arrive. Paul suggested that we should take advantage of our time in the building, so we asked Christina if we could go down into the basement. She agreed. As the team made its way to the elevator, I could already see apprehension on some of their faces. Christina slid the doors open and we all piled in.

"I still get a bad feeling in here. I prefer the stairs," Amanda J. said.

"I don't really like this elevator," Amanda K. added.

In the archive the camera recorded the banging stopping and a humming sound starting.

The elevator came to a stop and Christina pushed open the doors. We cautiously exited onto the cold concrete floor. I stood back and watched them. I could tell what most were thinking by their body language; although they didn't like the elevator, they were equally unsure of entering this subterranean place.

I held the team back and allowed Amanda K. to take the lead. This was her first time down there, and I was looking for insight into any activity she might perceive. I watched as she moved slowly from area to area, making her way to the long service hallway. She stopped abruptly.

"Are you okay?" I asked her.

"I just felt a whoosh of energy pass through me. I don't want to go in there. I don't know why, but they are telling me not to go in there," she said, looking towards the hall.

"Who is telling you?" I asked.

"I'm getting an image of a man. His skin is all burned." We paused for a few moments. "There are a few men down here."

Back in the archive the hum faded away. There was a rattling sound, then a male EVP said, "Danny."

Another male replied, "Yeah."

We entered the hall, and Amanda K. pointed out an orb visible to the naked eye, which passed us quickly and vanished.

"There is a dog down here, all scraggly, grey and beige hair. He has a collar and looks like Benji, only bigger."

After a walk around we headed back to the elevator. It was time to head upstairs to meet Michele and Darrin.

In the archive there was banging near the camera and movement directly behind it. An EVP of a male said, "Danny ... Danny."

Again, a male replied, "Yeah."

As we came to the service hall that led to the elevator, Amanda K. again stopped abruptly and focused on a space near a support pillar.

"What's going on?" I inquired.

"There is a very tall, hooded figure near the elevator. He is looking down and his eyes are hidden."

"What is he doing?"

"He will not look at me. I get that he is negative, and I'm getting the creeps from him. I can't read him at all," she said, staring at the spot.

I handed her the camera and asked her to take a photo of him. Although she tried several times, nothing was captured.

We gave the area a wide berth, just to be on the safe side, entered the elevator and headed up to the main floor.

As we waited for the arrival of the rest of the team, I wondered about the figure in the basement. I have considered the existence of grim reapers for many years, and I had to wonder if this cloaked figure could be one. It seems that the reaper represents an opportunity for the dead, for at the time of their death an individual has a choice to make: stay where they are (if trying to work out a problem) or move to a better place (please see the ghost experience chapter in this book).

The reaper seems to work on some type of schedule, returning for those who have refused to move on and giving them the chance to change their minds. You see, personal choice is truly the only gift we have in this life and the next.

They are extremely patient, always watchful, and faster than a heartbeat. The grim reapers have their eyes on each of us. They know we will all have a turn at shaking their hand one day as they lead us to the river. There is no cheating death.

The reaper is as old, if not older than humankind. Reapers have been assigned by the guy riding the pale horse (Death) to collect and guide us as we shed our physical selves. I believe they are more guides for the dead than collectors of souls, and this comes from the great many hauntings I have investigated. If a reaper had collected all these souls, I wouldn't have anything to investigate.

He is not alone, but one of an army of reapers working just beyond our perception, shadowed in mystery and symbolism.

It was not until the fifteenth century that we started to paint a terrifying picture of the reaper: a skeletal figure in a long black cloak carrying a scythe and sometimes an hourglass, all symbolic of death and our mortality. The skeletal image comes from a time when the plague ate its way through Europe, and people associated death with rotting bodies. The cloak represents an air of mystery, since Death could come unnoticed at any time. The scythe is to assist in reaping the souls for Death's harvest, and the hourglass shows us that our finite time here will certainly run out.

But are they out there?

After so many years of chasing the dead, I have on occasion had the opportunity to run into people, albeit extremely rare, who have seen and even spoken with a reaper and lived to talk about it. Many years ago, I had the pleasure of meeting a gifted young man who had the ability to see and hear things that most of us cannot. He had heard that I studied the paranormal and approached me. He wanted to know if what he was experiencing was normal, and he thought that perhaps he was crazy. I assured him that he wasn't. We had long discussions on these topics, and he told me about a recent experience.

Michael always began his psychic episodes with a migraine. Along with the pain in his head, he felt a darkness descend upon him. He was sitting at a window seat on a train heading to Toronto from out west, and although there were many passengers around him, he felt alone. Michael looked out of the window as the train lurched from the station. He peered down at the people going about their business on the platform below and thought, "Lucky people" — lucky because they were not riding this train.

As he nursed his headache, he saw a scenario playing out in his mind's eye, and he knew he would be okay. He leaned over to speak to the young woman beside him. He told her something was about to happen and not to worry. He would get her off the train. In retrospect, Michael acknowledged that what he had said made him seem crazy and must have frightened the woman, but at the time he didn't care, since he was focused on a solid black figure gliding along the aisle towards the front of the train. He remembered that as the train moved forward, it rocked from side to side, but this figure was not affected by the motion and moved in a perfectly straight line.

A few moments later Michael remembered the panic as the train rolled onto its side, and people and luggage were tossed everywhere. The young woman who had been sitting next to him landed on the windows on the other side of the train and broke her leg. Michael ended up carrying her to safety.

To add to the strangeness of this story, I happened to personally know the engineer driving the train that day. Afterward, I went to speak with him about the accident. He told me the trip had started out like any other. He was driving the train and had an assistant and a trainee with him in the engine. His partner told him to go take a rest. He would show the trainee around. The engineer agreed, relinquished his seat to the assistant, and left the engine to head to the meal car. Just as he sat down to lunch, the train derailed, twisting onto its side. Although there were many injuries, the only fatalities were the assistant and the trainee in the engine compartment.

Almost ten years ago, I met a distinguished gentleman named Dave who confided in me a story that disturbs him to this very day. Dave has a heart problem and had a pacemaker implanted. Unfortunately, the pacemaker failed several times, until it was replaced with a newer, more reliable version. Each time it failed, Dave went into cardiac arrest. It was late one evening, and he was at home with his wife when the device failed. Luckily, the response of the paramedics was quick. They kept him alive and rushed him to the hospital, where the doctors worked to restart his heart. It was at this point that Dave had a near-death experience. He could see his body on the table and the doctors and nurses milling around it. He could hear them talking and barking out orders. While he was standing there watching, a man in black approached him and told him he should come with him, since it was time to go. Dave refused, saying it was not his time, and he needed to get back to his body.

While they were arguing (Dave was and still is a stubborn person), another man dressed in black appeared and intervened. He asked for Dave's full name, including his middle name, which Dave provided. At that moment Dave felt a rush of pain and opened his eyes to the caring faces of the doctors and nurses looking down on him. He drifted off and was sent to the ICU to recover.

Late the next day, Dave received some bad news. Unknown to him, his ill elderly father had been brought to the same hospital only moments before Dave himself had arrived by ambulance. While Dave was being saved, his father had passed away. Dave told me that they shared the same first and last name, the only difference being the middle name. Did Death almost make an error? What might have happened had Dave not been so adamant about staying?

In another incident, a couple named John and Trish were heading home in rain that was turning the roads icy. John lost control of the vehicle, and the car plunged off a bridge. The horrific accident was over in a blink and left John dead and Trish badly injured. She somehow managed to crawl from the wreckage to find help. She told rescue workers that there was another person with John in the car. They conducted their search to no avail, later confirming that John and Trish were the only ones in that car. Could the other person momentarily perceived by Trish have been a reaper?

There isn't a great deal of information on encounters with reapers, but this may stand as testimony to their efficiency. I am sure there are other stories out there. Some have not been told in a public forum, some incidents may have never been understood, and then there are the experiences of people who do not believe in reapers. That's okay, because they believe in us, and in the end that's all that will matter. So as the Blue Öyster Cult says, "Don't fear the reaper."

It could be that reapers check in from time to time, looking for those who have come to realize they can now let go of the negatives and move on to a happier time.

After our possible reaper encounter, several of us headed outside to wait for Darrin and Michele. As we exited the building, Linda arrived, followed a few minutes later by Darrin and Michele.

Meanwhile, up on the third floor Amanda J. was sitting in the hall near the doorway to the archives. She heard shuffling sounds, muted banging, and a male voice, but she could not tell what he was saying.

In the back of the archive, an EVP of a male said, "Get out." There was tapping on the camera, the sound of a door opening, and then an EVP of a male saying, "Get out."

We all headed upstairs and I introduced Michele to Amanda K. They instantly hit it off. Michele later told me that although Amanda K. was young, Michele saw her as an old soul.

I directed the team into the back of the archives, allowing Michele and Amanda K. to lead us into the stacks.

"There is a man here in his thirties, brown hair," Amanda K. told us.

"He seems older, pain in the head, and shuffles around. I keep hearing Mark," Michele added.

"They are so timid," Amanda K. reported.

"Very shy." Michele nodded. "Somebody is here. I heard a *Shhh* sound." Amanda K. sensed the same thing.

Amanda J. heard footsteps deeper inside the archives.

Out in the hall, someone was calling Danny over and over, and there was the sound of something heavy being dragged across the floor, but the camera detected nothing.

We moved to the back stairs leading to the mezzanine level. Michele was in the lead but hesitated, then started up the stairs with Amanda K., Peter, and myself. Michele called down to us, "There are two men up here. One is having a cigarette."

A hint of tobacco smoke filtered past us.

"Oh, one is wearing a hat and the other has dark hair slicked back. They're workers, they wear coveralls," Amanda K said.

"They aren't seeing us. Looks like they're just up here having a break. I'm getting a Larry or Leonard and a Steve or Stanley," Michele explained.

As they turned to head back down the stairs, Michele unexpectedly peered over the side and almost fell, looking dizzy. "Someone fell off a scaffold here," she told us.

The team worked through the stacks and into the hall. Christina stayed back, searching for something.

The camera in the archive recorded an EVP of a female saying, "They are leaving now." There was a male reply, content unknown.

Bells rang and a male said, "Danny." There was whispering.

"I have a pain in my right knee," Amanda J. told Michele.

"You are picking that up from the guy I normally see passing through here. He has an injury to his right knee."

As we stood in the hall, Paul saw a ball of light pass through the door of Creative Services, cross the hall, and go through the closed door to the gym.

Amanda J. started off towards the far stairway and looked back at Michele, who followed, bringing Amanda K. with her.

"Every time I come into this building I end up in this stairway, and each time I hear music," Amanda J. told them.

"I hear it too," Michele said.

Amanda K. nodded.

Michele pulled a gauss meter from her pocket. She pointed it at several electrical sources and took a small reading from each. She pointed it at Amanda J. and it lit up to yellow. As she moved it away it returned to normal. We couldn't explain why each time the meter was pointed at Amanda J., it produced a high yellow reading.

Christina came out into the hall carrying two old photographs from the 1930s. "Is there anyone you recognize in these pictures?" she asked.

Michele took the first one and then handed it to Amanda K. The second one showed several hydro workers huddled in a group. Michele studied it for a moment then picked two men she believed were the ones in the mezzanine. The photo was then handed over to Amanda K., who looked at all the faces, paused for a moment then picked the same two men.

Unfortunately, the names of the men were not with the photo, but it was still remarkable that they had both picked the same two.

Linda suggested some coffee, so we decided to take a break. Linda and Christina headed through the stacks towards the kitchenette. A male EVP said, "Oh oh."

Peter headed back towards the stacks and met Linda and Christina. They brought the coffee to the office on a cart. Whispering followed them.

Once everyone had left the archive, it grew quiet. Then there was an EVP of a male saying, "Laurie!"

A female replied, "Yeah?"

The same male said, "Camera." It was shocking to hear a spirit warn another spirit of the presence of our surveillance equipment.

After the break, we headed down the hall to the elevator and back to the basement. As we rode the elevator, Amanda K. filled Michele in on the hooded figure. "There is a real creepy guy down there. I saw him earlier."

"Who is he?" Michele asked.

"I couldn't read him. He was very negative, and he was wearing a robe that hid his eyes."

"We can see if he is still there."

"I feel that he is still around somewhere."

At that moment Peter's digital recorder captured a male EVP making a sound as if he were amused.

The elevator stopped, and we disembarked into the basement.

Amanda K. looked around. "I don't see him now."

A male EVP on Peter's digital said, "Ah, think I'll go and eat."

Michele turned a corner near the cage. "Why is there smoke down here?"

No one else could see the smoke, so the team fanned out to investigate the floor.

As she neared the long hallway, Amanda J. mentioned that her eyes had started to burn and water, and she felt a tightness in her chest that made it hard to inhale to the point where she became lightheaded.

Paul called me over to where he was standing about ten feet from the cross corridor.

"What have you got?" I asked.

"What's this?" He held up his camera.

I looked into the viewfinder and saw a distinct bluish electrical band similar to a lightning bolt, stretching from the ceiling to the floor. I looked at the area but could see nothing, yet there it was in his viewfinder. Thinking it was a trick of light, I stepped away from him and looked through my camera — there it was shimmering between the floor and ceiling.

We both attempted to take photos of it but had no luck. We even moved positions, and although it remained, we just could not photograph it.

I thought back to the column of light Paul, Amanda J., and I had seen in the Barracks. It was very similar, although this one we could not see with the unaided eye. Could this have something to do with reapers? Was this the way out, a doorway? There was no way to know.

Michele and Amanda K. moved to the cage gate, and the team gathered around them, looking into the shadows beyond.

"Michael, is that you? Oh, why are you still here?" Michele asked. "You don't need to stay here anymore."

Amanda J. moved in closer. "I see flashes of red, movement with red."

"That's him," Michele told her. "It's okay, you can come forward."

"I see a dark shape moving on the right," Amanda J. said, falling back a step as she caught a glimpse of a face in the darkness.

Darrin stepped in close to the gate and pointed his camera into it, turning on his spotlight.

"He doesn't like that!" Michele warned.

Darrin pulled back and shut his light off.

Amada J. saw fog or smoke.

Michele put her hand up to the gate. "I see bars here, like a prison."

He was showing her something symbolic, something that's holding him to this place, I thought.

"I see the fence blurring, stretching out," Amanda J. said.

"I see it also," Amanda K. said, stepping in closer.

"It is so weird. There are bars here. It's like he is trying to pull me into this," Michele said, moving back from the gate.

"Harriet, I see the image of a woman. She is in her kitchen lying on the floor, crying. In her hand she holds a ring ... a wedding ring. There is so much guilt," Amanda K. said.

Was this image his wife or wife-to-be? Because he had passed so young and what could have been never was, could this be the guilt that held him here? Did he feel he'd missed out on everything life had to offer? Possibly. We stood there for a while longer until the images faded away.

Meanwhile, in the archive the camera picked up the sound of ringing bells. An EVP of a male said, "Danny … where are we next week?" Bells rang again. There was the sound of a door opening. "Get back, Danny!"

"Go have a peek, Danny." There was a strange walking-type sound, not like shoes heel to toe, but rather slap, slap, slap.

An EVP male yelled, "Danny!"

This was recorded on both cameras, and considering that they were at least sixty-five feet apart, it must have been very loud. As a matter of fact, the moment of the yell was loud enough that it startled a mouse in the main hallway, which fled to a hiding place.

An EVP of a male said, "Pat."

Another male replied, "I'm here, Danny."

The team regrouped and we headed up to the second floor.

We entered the second floor, and someone pointed to a wall in the hallway. There, printed on a piece of paper taped to the wall, was a drawing of a ghost. In big letters it said "Ghost crossing." Everyone had a chuckle.

"There is a man. He's well dressed, with deep-set eyes and salt-and-pepper hair. He seems frustrated, he's talking to himself and pacing. He is either an architect or builder. He was in charge of building something. The people who put the money up wanted it one way but he did it another," Amanda K. reported.

The team examined the floor, and Michele felt there was a child, a boy who ran around near some of the front offices near the washroom.

Neither Michele nor Amanda K. perceived any further activity on this floor, so we moved on to the third floor.

There were sounds of things being dragged in the hallway then whispers near the camera. All was quiet as the team went through the hall.

As we entered the archives, Linda had a surprise for us. In the hallway was a small door. When she pulled it open, stretched out before us were long grey metal stairs to a hidden mezzanine below. After thirteen months of investigation and countless times in this building, it was the first time I'd seen this area. We climbed down to an area with a mesh grate floor that looked like it was used as a change room. Off to the left was another set of stairs that led down to a storeroom, where supplies and new uniforms were kept. We went to the bottom and looked around. I saw an orb move near Christina, swirl around her, and then vanish.

Everyone moved back up to the mezzanine, pausing there. Around the room were several lockers, boxes of uniforms, two small tables, and three chairs, one of which was sitting in the middle of the floor.

"It's powerful up here," Michele said.

"It's like downstairs," Amanda K. added.

"Yeah, yeah. There is someone here, a male. He's hiding in the shadows. He won't come any closer though," Michele said, stepping forward.

Amanda K. tried to coax him out, and Peter's digital recorder captured a male voice, content unknown.

"Why won't you come forward and speak with us?" Michele asked.

Michele said the spirit was saying "Derigative." We all paused, trying to figure out what that meant.

Michele cocked her head to the side. "What do you mean?" she asked.

Peter stepped up. "I think he means 'derogatory.'"

Michele and Amanda K. laughed. Peter's digital recorded what sounded like a male becoming angry, but the content was difficult to confirm in the static that was coming from nowhere.

"What do you mean, 'derogatory'?" Michele asked.

"Do you still see him?" Peter asked.

Another strong burst of static hit Peter's digital recorder.

"He is fading away. There was another man standing over ... he is coming over to sit in the chair," Michele said, motioning to the chair in the middle of the floor.

"He is sitting down," Amanda K. confirmed.

Michele passed her meter over the chair, and it lit up.

"I just got a spike on my gauss meter here as well," Peter said.

"Who are you? Why are you here?" Michele asked, moving in closer to the chair.

There was a male voice recorded so low that we could not determine what was being said.

Peter's gauss meter started ticking to three milligauss.

"Is there someone there right now?" Peter asked, stepping in closer as well.

"He's right here," Michele replied.

There was a sound from the chair, like a movement, which we all heard.

"Here we go. Did you hear that?" Peter asked.

He was standing over the chair now, waving the gauss meter in what was more than likely right in the spirit's face. His digital recorder was hit with a burst of static, and in the static in a male's voice sounded angry.

The chair moved by itself with a loud scrape over the metal grating of the floor, and both Peter and Michele backed up.

"Whoa, okay he didn't like that," Michele said.

"He's leaving," said Amanda K.

Michele turned and looked back into the shadows. "Yeah, he's going."

We took a moment to absorb what had happened.

"Okay, let's go," I said, and the team climbed the stairs back up to the archive.

It had been an interesting night, but it was late and our time was just about up. I wanted to take Amanda K. to the exterior of the building to see what she might get back there.

As Peter, Alex, and I packed up the equipment, Amanda K. went to Christina in the office. "You need to find ledger 258," Amanda K. said. Christina looked for ledger 258, but it was listed as missing. This ledger held the names of workers.

We packed up the equipment, loaded everything into the car, then we all walked around the General Services Building to the rear work yard.

As we neared the back area, Amanda K. looked slightly to the right. "There is a fight going on, and not a very fair one. That guy is a lot bigger."

We stopped directly behind the building.

"Anything?" I asked her.

"Oh I see lots of blood, lots of bodies lying around everywhere. There are men with knives on the end of ... guns, they are walking around stabbing the ones lying down, stabbing the bodies. They're making sure they are dead." She was seeing events further back than I thought anyone could go. "There is a soldier here. He's saying he is from a regiment. He hasn't passed over. He has a large wound in his stomach," Amanda said, pointing to her right abdomen.

"What regiment?" I asked.

"You have to move on. It's okay, everything will heal when you move on … first." Her eyes were closed and she started to sway. "He is gone."

Did she say first? The 1st York regiment was one of the regiments at the Fort under the command of Major General Roger Hale Sheaffe.

There was nothing further, everyone was now tired. I thanked Linda and Christina for allowing us their time, I thanked the team for all their hard work, and as I walked quietly to my car, I thanked the many spirits here for putting up with my intrusion. This had been truly a remarkable journey for me. It reaffirmed to me that no matter what you know, or think you know, there will always be something new to learn. I had walked amongst so many opportunities here. To be wrapped in the fabric of history and see it as it was, be it in all of its glory or even at its ugliest, I had not looked away but embraced it for what it was. These were the lives lived so many years ago, and these were the events that had been created with their love and hate and blood and tears, and I felt in some small way that I was part of it all. I had a better understanding of most of what I had seen and heard over the last thirteen months, but I also realized that it wasn't over. The story was only half written — the lives and events that will succeed me have yet to take place. They will in the future only add to this story of work and tragedy and determination and achievement, for that is the true spirit of Exhibition Place.

Parting Thoughts

The grounds and buildings at Exhibition Place are some of the most fascinating haunted places I've had the privilege of investigating. Each building brought something new, and I think I can speak for the team when I say it pushed the envelope on challenges we had to overcome. The sheer size of a lot of these buildings at first led me to believe finding ghosts would be near impossible, a belief I now know was wrong. The abundance of spirit activity was overwhelming as we tried to keep recorded data separated from one spirit to the other in hopes of identifying as many as we could — not so easy in a place that is drenched in this much history.

THE GENERAL SERVICES BUILDING

The General Services Building proved to be extraordinary in that there were multiple spirits inhabiting the facility. Several of the spirits that we encountered had every reason to be haunting the building, since they had a deep connection to it. It was other spirits that showed up and seemed to be random, with no apparent connection to the building at all, that provided the greatest mystery.

They seemed to have died near or on the grounds, such as the deaths directly behind the General Services Building. This may also include deaths that occurred at the squatter houses and shacks that once existed just north of the building. For whatever reason, it would seem these transient visitors to the facility had chosen to stay. I had to wonder if the hydro vaults and the electromagnetic fields they produced were not somehow like a beacon drawing spirits from the surrounding area. In any case, the spirits there seemed friendly and social, save the two who have deeper, more dramatic messages to tell about themselves.

It was interesting to see that where the hydro worker was killed, a gate was built to enclose the area. I have to wonder if the worker connected to the staff in a subconscious way and communicated that the area was dangerous, and they in turn secured the area with a gate and padlock.

STANLEY BARRACKS

Stanley Barracks was interesting in the sense that there were multiple hauntings segregated into small pockets. There seemed to be individuals roaming the building, and there were small groups like the father and his daughter Jenny on the first floor, who never really became involved with the other spirits.

There was the group in the basement that was not only extremely negative to each other, but to us as well.

Although there seemed to be many layers or time frames of haunting occurring in this building, very few seemed to be from its long military past. Most of them seemed quiet and content, and some appeared to be still carrying out their deep commitment to duty. However, the problem seems to stem from the co-op inhabitants between 1947 and 1953.

Bob and David rule their small part of the Barracks, and they play their game very well. The danger is that David appears to do whatever Bob asks of him, allowing Bob to hide in the shadows. We feel if push comes to shove, Bob would not hesitate to sacrifice David for his own cause, which could spell real disaster for the living. It would also appear that there is no sanctuary for the other spirits who have little option but to deal with these two, but I believe that if or when Bob and David try to expand their power base within this building, they will run into Jenny. Depending on how they play out that scenario, it could bring disaster, as I feel that Jenny's father, being an old soldier, may turn the tables on Bob and David. Should this occur, it could translate into phenomena that the living will undoubtedly hear and feel.

THE HORSE PALACE

The Horse Palace was extremely interesting. A great deal of activity was witnessed but little proof was collected. It is as if the spirits there knew how to keep their secrets. The restaurant was a completely different story. The spirits there didn't seem shy at all, and the one running the bar hinted about having a sense of humour, albeit a strange one.

I was incredibly fascinated by some of the EVPs collected. The spirits made it clear that not only did they know they were dead, but they were aware of us and they commented specifically on team members and what we were doing. Although I had seen this happen once before in the thirty-something years I've been doing these investigations, I had believed it to be extremely rare. I was shown to be wrong when several were recorded, two in the Horse Palace itself.

THE CIVIC ARENA

This building was one of our greatest challenges due to its sheer size, but it produced a great deal of activity, with everyone in attendance experiencing not only strange events and visible apparitions but also physical contact. Most of the spirits that dwell in this beautiful building do not know they are dead and seem to go about their daily business. This includes the person who tumbled off the upper deck.

THE CRYSTAL PALACE/HORTICULTURE BUILDING

Although the team was not granted access to conduct an investigation, there are plenty of eyewitness reports and historical events to provide enough confidence that this building is extremely haunted.

THE PRESS BUILDING

The spirits here seem to have a dutiful purpose, as if they are performing the same roles in death as they had in life. There were a few instances where they did interact with us, which were observed in our EVPs, but most of the activity appeared to be the sounds and conversations you would find in any given office today. However, again there was one who was well aware that they are dead and commented directly on the team and its activities.

THE QUEEN ELIZABETH BUILDING

Although our investigation here was cut short, the activity and spirits in this building troubled me, as there was little doubt that they knew they were dead. They seemed to almost command ownership over the building and had little regard for the living. They, in my personal opinion, displayed characteristics teetering on dangerous. They reminded me somewhat of Bob and David from the Barracks, but where Bob and David were thugs, these spirits struck me as having a sense of class.

SCADDING CABIN

Being the oldest structure on the grounds, the cabin was interesting. The team speculated on who the sobbing woman might have been, but it was nothing more than speculation. Had we captured more, we might have been able to narrow down who she was, but due to the building's extremely long history and the fact that some of the buildings on the grounds have displayed transient spirits, it would be impossible to even hazard a guess as to what her identity was and what time frame she fits into. What was really interesting were the images Peter had captured as the team neared the cabin. Was it something from the history of the cabin, from the fort, or could it have been something else?

THE BANDSHELL

What a beautiful piece of architecture. I would have liked to have gone back for further investigation, but as it stands this building seems not to be haunted.

THE GROUNDS

The grounds have so many stories of people hearing and seeing strange things. Given the history of this land and all the events that have taken place here, it isn't a surprise that it would be saturated with many souls.

THE MILITARY CEMETERY

This piece of land is truly remarkable, and the spiritual energy that gravitates here is immeasurable. I believe there are paranormal occurrences here on a daily basis, and most people have passed them by without even noticing. As strange as that may sound, I think the energies that manifest do so in ways that convince people that the person they just saw by that tree or on that bench is real, living flesh and blood.

—/—

It was interesting that both mediums had detected very similar activity and spirits. For example, they both discovered Michael in the General Services Building and how he had died, pulling very specific information from him. The murder that took place there was also seen by both. They also found psychic details of fire and smoke which turned out to historically correct, and they both saw a dog that we captured on EVP. Michele and Amanda K.'s talents are remarkable.

Paul made some very interesting observations about how the camera was being influenced by something unseen, and when he took the time to dig deeper, he made the connection that the same phenomena were occurring when the team passed the camera lens, causing the iris to self-adjust. This is an important discovery, as it tells us that the camera in some restricted way detects the spirit as it passes by, but for reasons unknown the data is not translated to our recording system. This information will allow us to develop field experiments and important equipment modifications for the future.

He also came up with a viable theory on who or what Danny was based on exhaustive analysis of specific EVPs.

With so much spirit activity taking place, one may never know when they are about to have a remarkable encounter from the rich history of such an incredible place. To get that rare peek into another reality most only see in history books would be something unforgettable.

Appendix I

From the Team and Participants

I wanted to provide a forum for those who had something more to say about the investigations, observations, and encounters at Exhibition Place. This is what they had to say in their own words.

This was the biggest job we have ever done, and there were a great many challenges for us to overcome. It is such a great place, with so much history and so much going on. There were so many memorable moments — being the first one to see and hear things we had captured on surveillance was a real thrill, and you just never knew what would come next. The most memorable experience without doubt was at the Military Cemetery when the clairvoyant was talking about injustices there, and a coin came out of nowhere and hit me in the back. To find it was a coin from 1812 with Lady Justice on it was truly remarkable.

Paul Palmisano

The investigations were incredible. I had no idea what to expect, but after walking through the buildings in search of ghostly energies, I was pleasantly surprised to find many. I was able to establish clear communication and in some cases strong physical contact with many different entities.

One memorable experience was in the Stanley Barracks, where I was attacked by two very negative spirits. I was scratched on my back once in the basement hallway and another time in the woman's washroom. It was scary and painful, but at the same time I was excited to have such activity happen that could be witnessed and documented.

Michele Stableford

It was the last night The Searcher Group would be going to investigate at the Barracks, and Michelle and I went along to help. Richard had shown Michelle and I quite a few unexplained pictures from their previous visits, and we made it our mission to investigate each spot to see if we could find reasonable explanations for all of them. Michelle had been to the Barracks once before and wanted to have nothing to do with the creepy bathroom in the basement. Well, guess what, I had to go to the bathroom. I have never seen such a horrified look on Michelle's face as when Richard asked her to accompany me there. Thankfully, nothing happened, but that look will be forever imprinted in my mind ... priceless. Aside from that funny memory, I will also never forget talking with Michelle and Christina outside one of the rooms when we heard a woman moaning, almost screaming. The three of us looked around. There was no one except Richard and a few others standing in a group about ten feet away. At first I thought it had been one of them but then realized they were all men, and none of them would have been able to imitate a woman so accurately. By the end of the evening Michelle and I could not find reasonable causes for all the strange pictures that had previously been taken.

Sarah Angeles

I was walking along the tree line in the Military Cemetery. As I was nearing the bridge above us, there between the two closest trees I saw a black shadow. It appeared as though there was somebody leaning against the tree, since the shadow was slanted. As I moved closer to get a better look, the shadow darted through the trees towards the bridge, disappearing. I followed, and as I walked into the scrub, I saw nothing but felt a strong presence; there was no one else around me.

Jonathan Wallace

I'm as psychic as a brick (which is not helpful when the subject of the paranormal fascinates me as much as it does), so for several years I have desired to experience first-hand evidence of paranormal phenomena, without much success. Time spent investigating what is left of the Stanley Barracks with The Searcher Group did not disappoint. I was amazed that a medium who had been viciously clawed by a male spirit had returned as part of our group, a week later. "Back for more, are ya?" I quipped as I introduced myself to Michele. In hindsight, her persistence — as well as that of *all* the members of The Searcher Group — spoke volumes of the seriousness with which true paranormal investigation is conducted.

To make a long night shorter, let me attest to the activity I witnessed that evening, first-hand. Distinct knockings were heard by all seven investigators present, in direct response to questions asked aloud in the women's washroom (located in the basement). During this same period of questioning, Michele was once again attacked — this time kicked hard in the small of her back. As Richard and I rushed to her aid, she lifted the back of her shirt to reveal a heel imprint forming in red, on her left side. After taking a few moments to recover, Michele valiantly defied her invisible attacker and continued to stand her ground, as did everyone present.

A digital recording I made of the otherwise empty washroom revealed more phenomena during a fifteen-minute break period. While the team congregated two floors above, the recorder picked up multiple knockings (similar to those heard and recorded by the group earlier), footfalls, distant wails of pain (as if in response to a lashing or beating), and crinkling of the baby powder-covered plastic bag that was purposely left on the floor to capture imprints in our absence. Upon closer review of this recording, an unmistakable wail echoes further down the hall from the washroom, as if in response to my discussing the death of the infant.

My experiences during an investigation at the Horse Palace proved just as interesting. As Richard left the group to use the restroom behind the bar, five of us heard the unmistakable footfalls of someone wearing high heels following him, passing the men's room door and entering the women's room door, a few yards further along. We investigated, finding no one present in the women's washroom and surprising Richard, who had been oblivious to his like-minded spectral pursuer and wondered why, as he emerged from the men's room, the rest of his team was now filing out of the ladies room!

My audio recordings from the Horse Palace include a child's voice from among the rows and rows of upper floor stables and the rants of one or two unsavory-sounding male entities, one of whom actually asks, "You don't see me? I'm right here!" The implications one may take from this captured phenomena are staggering.

The grounds of what is now Exhibition Place are most definitely haunted. There are memories embedded in the atmosphere there so strongly, time is powerless to dissolve them. There are intelligent energy forms that have left the realm of the physical and continue to visit and reside there. We have only begun to hear their stories, and I am grateful to have been a part of the collecting of them.

Peter Roe

We had entered a higher level in one of the buildings we were investigating — a large room with several sectioned off, fenced-in areas. I had lingered behind slightly, and as I heard the group get ahead, I walked back to join them, skimming along the border of a fenced wall. Michele and Sheryl were chatting before they looked over at me. I got a bad feeling as they grinned kind of menacingly and told me I should try walking through the centre of the area I had just passed, towards a fire extinguisher on the far wall. Hesitantly I turned and started to walk forwards. I only took a few steps, feeling no uneasiness, then took another confident step forward before stopping dead in my tracks. A sudden breeze hit my face, and my eyes and face flushed warmly. I quickly turned around, saying, "I don't think so …" explaining what had just happened as they laughed, nodding knowingly. We then decided to have the female team members join hands, combining energy to see if we could pick up on anything. As we held hands, my body and face grew much warmer, making my eyes sting a little even as they were closed. I soon got the feeling of someone beside me on my right, since that side felt much cooler than my left. As Michele was speaking, I felt a few light pokes against my right arm, then a light brush against my right cheek. Michele then questioned the energies about long hair, and she and I each felt slight tugs at our hair, mine near the top of my head. When asked for a name, I sensed a "Bryan," and Michele said "There's a Ben." She said she had picked up on a "Ryan" earlier, so I might have just heard a combination of the two names. As communication dwindled down, we moved to leave the level. I had been so preoccupied in my thoughts about what had just happened that I went to move through the same spot as before, towards the fire extinguisher. I suddenly gasped as I re-experienced what I had felt earlier, quickly turning to move away from the spot, almost bumping into Michele.

Amanda Jobe

I have always had an interest in ghosts and whether they are real. Some people would argue that there is no such thing as ghosts. However, sometimes "seeing is believing." I was given the opportunity to take part in a few investigations, and I went along not knowing what to expect. Since I was a "newbie" to this sort of thing, I was willing to get out there and see for myself. During one investigation I was sent to investigate the ladies washroom. Now, I would like to think there is a logical way to explain why the faucet turned on by itself, but I don't know how it did. It sent shivers down my back … and I couldn't stop my hands from shaking. From that moment on I knew I was not alone … someone wanted to communicate with me. The scariest time was when we were in Stanley Barracks and something touched me, something unseen. It was truly fascinating but also terrifying.

Anna deSousa

During an investigation I attended at Stanley Barracks, I witnessed something that I couldn't explain. I had arrived at the location before any of the other investigators. I walked around the building and personally noted that all the windows were closed. At the end of the night, we were surprised to see that a window was now open. Some of the investigators had taken photos prior to us entering the building that clearly show that this window was closed. These windows are very old and heavy, and it would be highly unlikely that wind could have blown it open. We know that no one had entered that section of the building, as it was off limits and alarmed.

Also that night I witnessed a medium trying to utilize a process known as automatic writing. This was something I was highly skeptical about. The medium was given a pen and a pad of paper. The theory is the spirit is able to use the medium's hand to write down responses to questions asked by others in the room. When she started this process, she appeared to go into a trance. Her hand started to move in circles on the page until a question was asked, and then a response was written. I was watching the pen and paper the entire time, and she always wrote the responses from left to right in big letters. Afterwards, during the review of the pad, I noticed that there were definitely responses written from left to right, but there were also words written vertically up and down using the entire length of the pages. I found this very interesting, as it is almost impossible to write something from left to right and up and down at the same time.

Grant MacPhee

So many things happened during the investigations that have made me a believer in the paranormal, from hearing whistling down an empty hallway to feeling the deep negativity, pain, and suffering of those who had died, or the rushes of cold air that I believe are from someone on the other side trying to get our attention. Although I have experienced such clear, audible encounters with spirits, it never ceases to amaze me that the souls of the dead still roam amongst us.

Jim Costa

I started working in the archives in 1989. Most of the odd things I heard I put down at first to things going on in the rest of the building or next door in the hydro yard that I didn't know about and couldn't see. For instance, just before the annual CNE, I would work late, sometimes till eleven p.m. On those nights, as I sat in my office, I would often hear what sounded like a large crashing noise in the storage area behind me. In fact, the crashing was so loud, I was usually convinced that a whole shelving unit had toppled. I'd race to the area, only to find everything in order. Years later, when I mentioned this to a colleague who worked down the hall in the sign shop, he said he often heard the same thing in his area, but he could never find any evidence of anything falling or breaking. Security staff, when on alone late at night, have also reported the sounds of things crashing around overhead (they are on the first floor and the archives and sign shop are on the second floor).

The first year I worked in the archives, I stayed overnight in the boardroom on the top floor a couple of times, as it got too late to even bother going home. Again, this was usually just before the CNE. Each time I stayed overnight, I heard footsteps in the hallway, virtually every hour. When I asked security how often they patrolled the top floor of the building, they said once, at eleven p.m. They also assured me that no one else was in the building on those occasions. At that point, they always said what most employees in the building say when something is unexplained: "It must be the ghost of GS." This had become a standard response to the many odd things that happen in the building. The ghost spoken of is assumed to be the night watchman who died in the building in the 1960s.

The night watchman mentioned above was given to whistling as he did his rounds, and several employees had heard this whistling, including me. I was in my office on a Sunday afternoon and heard someone whistling in the stairwell. I called downstairs to security and told them it wasn't funny, as I thought the two employees on shift had heard the stories about the whistling night watchman and were trying to scare me. Since they were relatively new employees, they hadn't heard the stories, and they assured me it hadn't been either of them. No one else was in the building. When I asked one of them to come up to my office and escort me downstairs (so I wouldn't have to walk through the stairwell alone), he sheepishly refused, as he was too scared to help me. I walked down alone without incident.

On several occasions, again around CNE time, I would get to the top floor of our building heading for the archives, when I would hear what sounded like a party taking place somewhere behind closed doors. The sound was muffled, but I could hear glasses clinking and men and women laughing. As I searched for the room housing the party, the sound would just dissipate. Even if I went back and stood where I had first heard the sounds, the party was gone. I chalked this up to a party going on outside until a colleague who worked in the Sign Shop reported the same thing. It was her first year working in the building, and she had come in to do the midnight to eight a.m. shift. She dreaded working in the building late at night and was pleased when she heard the party, since she thought it meant she wasn't alone on the floor. For her, the sound was like a bubble she walked through before she opened the door to the top floor. She was very displeased and frightened when she realized the party sounds had evaporated and that she was alone.

More recently, I have heard noise in the hallway while I work. It sounds like someone moving furniture or pushing large garbage bins across the floor. When I look, nothing is going on. A female member of the painting staff heard the same thing in the hallway late one night when she was using the women's washroom on the top floor. She looked in the hallway but nothing had moved; she immediately fled downstairs.

I also hear footsteps in the hallway when no one is there. One day, I heard the double doors halfway down the hall open and close, then I heard loud footsteps coming towards my office. I was convinced that this time it was a real person. I sat at my desk looking out to the hallway, waiting to see who it was. The footsteps came right to the door and stopped, and it was as if the person then turned to look into the office, but there was no one there.

After one of my staff saw a man dressed in black moving quickly through the main aisle of the archives, an odd thing happened that I put down to an overactive imagination that probably sprang from the sighting of the spirit in black. I was moving a skid of records in a tight passageway when something large and black moved quickly behind and somewhat over me. It made me duck and move forward. At first I thought someone had thrown something at or over me. But no one was there. I didn't think much of it until paranormal researchers using a digital camera found a similar black object flying through a storage area across the hall from where my incident occurred.

My only other odd experience came about three months ago, when I saw someone wearing a dark brown plaid shirt go into the room across the hall from my office. The door was open, since the area was being cleared out to give the archives more storage space. I got up from my desk and went to the room to see who it was. No one was there. When I tried to think of anyone who used to wear dark plaid shirts, it came to me that Hal, an elderly man who had worked in that room for years and who is now dead, always wore those kind of shirts. He probably wasn't happy about our clearing out his space and getting rid of his favourite sewing machine (he made bunting and banners for the CNE for years, as did others after him, but now the job has been outsourced, and that is how the archives got the room for its use).

As my 2009 summer student is no longer with us, I should relate her story as well. She was in the storage area when she heard a giggling child. Oddly, she suppressed what she had heard until a couple of days later, when we all started telling stories about things we'd seen or heard. It was like she had tried to forget and had hidden it away in some deep recess in her memory. It popped back out when our stories prompted her memory.

Linda Cobon, Manager,
Records and Archives, Exhibition Place

NIGHT WATCHMAN

In the late spring of 2007, when I was still a relatively new volunteer at the archives, I was working in the back stack area inspecting some films. I decided to listen to some music, as it is very quiet in the stack area. I was listening to a wide range of music, everything from big band to rock. Throughout the course of the day I could see movement out of my right side peripheral vision. Every time I looked over, nothing was there, so I thought it might be birds flying past the window. Finally, while the song "Bring Me to Life" by Evanescence was playing, I felt like someone to my right was watching me. I looked over to see what looked like a night watchman staring at me from about five feet away. He looked like a full person, but in soft focus. He was wearing a white shirt with black tie and black pants with black-rimmed glasses. As we looked at each other, he turned to his right and walked down one of the stack aisles. I turned back to what I was doing and tried to assess what just happened. After a few minutes, I turned off the music and told the archives manager about what I'd seen. She told me about a night watchman who had passed away on the job in this building a long time ago. She brought out a photo of him and asked if this was the man I saw. I confirmed that it was. She stated that lots of people (security mostly) had heard him around the building as if still on rounds, but no one had seen him. I don't know why he showed himself to me — maybe he didn't like the music I was listening to or he just wanted to let me know he was around. In either case, I don't listen to music in the back anymore.

WOMAN WITH CHILD AND MAN IN BLACK

A few weeks after the night watchman incident, I was inspecting film again when I saw a woman with a little girl walk down the main aisle of the back stack area. After they had passed me, a man in black came down the same aisle very quickly, as if wanting to catch up with them. The three didn't stop to look at me, and I don't know if they knew I was there. They were just walking through, as if trying to get somewhere. The woman was very clear and dressed in the style of the Gibson Girl or turn of the century. She wore long greyish skirt, a shimmery orange mutton-sleeved blouse, and a beautiful large hat. The little girl was hazy, but I could tell she was wearing a short little dress with a ribbon or bow in her hair. The man in black was moving very quickly and hazily, but he wore a black suit with what looked like a top hat.

I have seen the woman only one other time since the sighting above. It was in our archives office area. A co-worker was working on some old photos in Photoshop. I looked over to see the woman leaning over my co-worker's shoulder to see what she was working on. I wish I could have asked my co-worker what images she was working on, since it might have provided insight into who this lady is.

THE GIGGLING GIRL

Again, while in the back stack area working on the film collection, I heard what sounded like a little girl giggling. It didn't last very long, and I wondered if she liked the spinning film reels enough to make her laugh. I hope so.

OTHER RANDOM THINGS

When I'm in the back working on the film collection, I've often heard whistling. It seems to come from many different places, but mostly from the front area that separates location 1 from location 2. Once I recognized a tune and whistled it back, only to have it whistled back at me.

More often than I'd like to admit, while in the kitchen, I feel like I'm being watched. Sometimes I swear I hear someone walking towards the kitchen, not footsteps, but the sound of rustling clothes. The same is true for the women's washroom.

Sometimes when I'm working in the archives alone on Saturdays, I get the impression that I am not wanted in the back stack area, almost as if I'm invading or intruding on their space. I feel very uncomfortable and quickly leave.

Overall, I'd say that our friends in the back are friendly, and I try to respect them. When I'm the first one in or the last one to leave for the day and turn on or off the lights in the back, I either say good morning or good night to them, just as I would to a co-worker. When a walking tour comes through the stack area, I also let them know in advance, hoping this will ease their feelings.

Christina Stewart, Media Archivist,
Records and Archives, Exhibition Place

Appendix II

Skeptics and Cynical Skeptics

Skepticism is natural and healthy. It allows us to build logical arguments, conduct rational conversations, and can entertain forward thinking and new ideas.

Cynical skepticism is employed by people who are terrified of change, who are content in a society that they perceive has reached its ultimate potential and has nowhere further to go, or who have deep underlying motivation to ensure there are no changes or advancements in society or science. Nothing threatens their current belief system. These are the people who are devoted to the idea of the impossible. These were the same people who thought the idea of replacing horse-drawn carriages with motorized carriages was pure madness, or thought John F. Kennedy had gone mad and questioned if he was the right president to lead the country after his speech about putting a man on the moon. Let's not forget two scientists, Galileo and Bruno, who believed in Nicolas Copernicus's theories on astronomy and the heavens. Galileo was arrested and forced to renounce his beliefs, and Bruno was burned at the stake. Roger Bacon believed in the ways of science, and for those beliefs he served ten years in prison. His books were banned, by order of the Pope. Cynical skeptics arrange arguments on new thoughts and theory with ridiculous interjections, as though pulling absurd answers from a pretext and inserting them into dialogue like square pegs into round holes.

We need to avoid these people and connect with people who have a sense of logic and a healthy skepticism if we are going to move forward as a society and make meaningful discoveries, not just in life after death research, but in anything we do.

What is evidence?

Evidence can come in many forms, from material exhibits to testimony. In criminal law, these forms of evidence, when given in a reliable and reasonable form of information, can establish a true picture of what occurred. Evidence is either direct or circumstantial. When direct evidence is provided, it will normally show that the information is true beyond a reasonable doubt, for example fingerprints, DNA, and audio and video surveillance. Circumstantial evidence mainly supports a theory and can suggest proof but does not prove something unequivocally, as eyewitness testimony does. When a blend of direct and circumstantial evidence is provided, it can give a complete picture of the entire event.

Corroborating evidence is normally a combination of evidence collected from several sources that all points to the same event. For example, a bank camera records Joe crossing east on Main Street at 2:45. Frank bumped into a man fitting Joe's description on the east side of Main Street around the same time. Even though Joe claims he was not in the area, the corroborating evidence proves otherwise.

An expert witness is, by virtue of their specialized education, training, skill, or experience, believed to have expertise and specialized knowledge in a particular subject beyond that of the average person, making their opinion sufficient that others may rely on it.

We must look at all the information available in an attempt to answer the question of evidence. The evidence in most cases is circumstantial at best, that of a single witness to the phenomenon. There are, however, thousands of cases in the paranormal that are corroborated by multiple witnesses to a single event. Some of the best evidence comes from multiple witnesses supported by audio/video surveillance. In these cases there would be enough evidence to send an accused person to jail, but somehow it falls short of convincing people of the existence of the soul. If the judicial system was run by the cynical skeptic, no one would ever be incarcerated.

Appendix III

The Ghost Experience

Spirits haunt places that are familiar and have personal relevance to them. Most never show signs of that significance to the witness, but rather they are preoccupied with their own activity.

Do residual hauntings exist? This is a question I find myself asked quite often, especially at Exhibition Place, which is surrounded by such a rich and sometimes strange history.

The technical answer to this question is a complicated one, but the short answer is no.

A residual haunting is paranormal activity of sight or sound that occurs and re-occurs in the same manner each time without the ability to change, deviate, or interact. From the observer's point of view it seems like a recording being played of some past event. Most investigators make the distinction that a residual haunting is unlike an intelligent haunting, because it cannot deviate from its routine and cannot interact with the witness.

In this I agree, but I do profess that if the correct research is conducted on the location of the haunting, then it is very possible to interrupt the occurrence and possibly change the witnessed event.

One of the first people to suggest the theory that residual hauntings exist was Thomas Charles Lethbridge in his 1961 book *Ghost and Ghoul*. This was later popularized in a 1972 film by Peter Sasdy titled *The Stone Tape*, which followed the theory that past events could be recorded into rocks. Thus it became known as the "Stone Tape Theory."

It was believed and remains widely so that past events, and specifically traumatic events, can be absorbed and recorded into inanimate objects. It is suggested that limestone, quartz, and magnetite are the best candidates.

If this theory holds true, then it should be a matter of study to be able to find the method and means to play that recording at will, though this has never been accomplished. It has been further suggested that the proverbial replay button would be an observer's psychic ability, which causes the event to play out.

This hypothesis can be immediately ruled out, as I have investigated hundreds of haunted locations and am an avid user of electronic surveillance equipment, on which I have recorded events in locations purported to be those of residual hauntings. I mention this because most of the time I will record at a location where there is no living person, and therefore a psychic cause for a phantom occurrence would not be possible.

In my theory "The Memory Matrix," I explain that we are the sum of our memories. In death these memories assist our spirit in building a self-sustaining reality. It is within this reality that the power of the mind can cause remarkable phenomena.

Imagine for a moment that something very important happened to you. It could be very positive or very negative in nature, and it becomes such a powerful memory for you that you find yourself daydreaming about that event. The difference is when the un-insulated energy of the spirit has one of these powerful memories, it could expand its reality memory bubble and manifest independently from the spirit, thus giving the observer the impression that it is a type of recording. This would explain ghost ships and phantom trains as well.

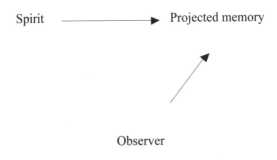

Even if one could witness this phenomenon in fine detail each time it occurred, it would be noted that small, seemingly insignificant, changes happened at each time this manifesting daydream was projected. The spirit would subtly alter things due to changes in memory or by inserting new information that either came to their mind or that they didn't like the last time they played through this memory.

So how did it all start to become a confusing mess?

After living in a haunted house as a child, as soon as I could read I was looking at all that I could on the subject of ghosts and hauntings. I was awestruck by those ghost hunters and parapsychologists who defied terror to seek out a spirit scaring the living out of their homes in the middle of the night. I looked up to them as leaders, my leaders in this quest to find the truth. There was only one thing to do. I was young, and I followed their theories with great enthusiasm. It wasn't until many years later, when I started conducting field investigations and experiments, that I ran into trouble. I wanted to learn how they manifested, where they existed, and most importantly, I wanted to know what elements combine to form what we perceive as an apparition. The trouble came as I tried to fit old theories into what my observations and data were telling me. There seemed to be some great conflict.

When I compared the theory to the observation, logic was nowhere to be found, and this became a perplexing conundrum. Was there no room for logic within parapsychology? Why? How could I continue my work, how could I apply any type of scientific method without a basis in logic? How could this happen? It took me more than a year to finally come to the conclusion that I had been led astray. I was discovering that most of these theories were indeed wrong, or simply misguided. I found this somewhat disheartening and yet at the same time quite exciting. It was a long road of discovery to understand why those before us would have led us in these directions. Looking back, it was these trusted people within society, pillars of the community, who were being called upon to answer impossible questions at a moment's notice. We have to understand that most were churchgoers or clergy and had a predisposed ideology concerning what was occurring, even before looking into the occurrences. In order to maintain their standing, they had very little choice but to provide some reasonable explanation for what they thought was taking place.

Imagine for a moment that there was a cry for help going out to some of the most revered people in the community, and the response was "We just don't know." They had to provide an answer. The beginning of the modern spiritual movement lay in those answers, and it was from those answers that theory was now built. Then came those who felt they could earn a living working in the field of parapsychology, churning out book after book on the subject. They ran with old theories, casting them in stone without any proof whatsoever. This caused great harm, since they professed these theories without any evidence, and the scientific community turned its back on the entire subject. For those who wanted to do work in parapsychology, there seemed to be but one starting point, the old theories. From them we compiled what looked like new theories, which were only extensions of the old ones, distorted and twisted to fit like a square peg into a round hole. This just added to the confusion and deepened the mystery. This was conformity at its worst. It helped sell books, and one never had to step out onto a ledge and take the chance of ridicule from other paranormal investigators. Most sit on the fence and silently wait for some trend to appear on the horizon, then they promote this idea as if it were their own.

The best example of the confusion we are faced with is what we call spirit energy. Entities, ghosts, spooks, specters, shades, apparitions, spirits, shadows, the list goes on and on. Even the term "poltergeist" has its own distinction. Each name carries with it its own attributes. Logically, if what we are studying is the soul of those departed, and every person acts and reacts completely different from the others, then how can we assign labels that distinguish each by their actions? Judging by the list, it is either far too long or far too short. I will always maintain that people are people; dead or alive, they will act and react as they are accustomed. Let's look at some of the ghosts we came across at Stanley Barracks, for example. David and Bob, what would we call them? Over the course of several investigations we have heard them, seen them, and recorded them. I suppose from the list we could say they are entities, but how about in the early part of the investigation, when we perceived them as fleeting shadows in our peripheral vision? We might have called them shadow people. Then they attacked Michele and Paul and moved our equipment, which was classic poltergeist activity. Since these encounters were with the same two ghosts, it would have confused the issue if we started to assign labels to them for each incident. It doesn't take much to see how easy it is for affairs to become ridiculous.

We are the sum of our memories and emotions. Memory is the building block of our mind and forms our personality. Memory is a collection of things learned about who we are and the world we live in, what we like or dislike, what our passions are, to the very fundamentals of where we live and work and how we get there each day. Memories are very closely attached to our emotions. Emotion varies in degrees and is greatly influenced by memory. For example, you run into that old friend from school you once had a crush on, and instantly memories will bring back a flood of emotions. Or if you see someone approaching who has caused you trouble, your emotion will determine if you stand your ground and give them a piece of your mind or find an escape route. When we die, our personality remains, carrying with it all of its memories and emotions. Although the spirit exists beyond our perception, it is those memories and emotions that cause locations to be haunted, and the causes of a haunting are as plentiful as those individual's memories and emotions. It could be that the spirit simply has a story to tell, or they were possibly a victim. Have you ever reacted to a situation or witnessed someone reacting to an event in a purely emotional outburst with little thought behind it? Most emotional outbursts are involuntary, simply witnessing an event and reacting to it. It can be as simple as hearing a song in the present that triggers a deep emotional memory from the past.

In one such case, just before Christmas in 1998, I was working with people who were experiencing ghostly phenomena in their home. The family and I were sitting in the kitchen having tea. In the adjacent living room (it was an open concept living space) a mixed tape of Christmas music was playing on the stereo. Midway through the tape, "Ave Maria" started playing, and the spirit of a small child (female) started to sing along from across the living room. Not only was it a moving experience, but we were all witness to this spirit manifesting in sound brought on by her own personal emotional memories of this song and what it represented to her during the holiday season.

After years of research, observation, and experiments, I have formed a theory that I call the Memory Matrix.

It would seem that when we die, we develop a completely new reality derived from our own memories. This reality is built of pure memory and will encompass where we lived, played, and worked. It will also include all the people not only that we were close to, but also everyone we ever met, living or dead. This new reality may not be a perfect representation of the individual's life history but rather as it was remembered by that individual.

The construction of the Memory Matrix, built from the individual's state of mind at the time of death, will determine if a haunting will commence.

There are many variables that factor heavily in the development of the Memory Matrix. The major factors can be positive, as when the individual has no lingering issues, they are content and satisfied with their life, and they have no ill feelings with regard to anyone. This individual will revert to a deeply beautiful time that brought them the most joy in their past life. They will be peaceful, and the living will never perceive them. On the other hand, it could be negative, when the individual had caused harm to others and feels they may face persecution, they committed suicide, they were a victim or held a deep obsession regarding a relationship, money, property, or things they were involved with that were unjust or unresolved. Because most of these negatives remained deeply ingrained at the end of their life, this will allow them to maintain a new reality within their own Memory Matrix that exists very close to our own reality, and can therefore cause ghostly activity perceived by the living.

The dead who are negative may cause hauntings for many reasons, such as they have a story to tell about being a victim, they may not like us being in their home, or they may simply be forcing their morals on us. For example, someone who died back in the forties or fifties, belonged to a church, and was devoted to that era's moral standards may be upset with an unwed couple moving in and sleeping together. This person would find it difficult to communicate their feelings, so they would simply use methods available to them to evict the couple, which normally translates into terror for the living.

But how do they manifest?

At times, in every person's life, emotions can be so intense, they may become uncontrollable. I believe the trigger of a physical manifestation is the involuntary production of emotions. Thoughts, memories, or observed occurrences can easily create a dynamic response or reaction, even on a subconscious level. How we deal with emotion in life is no different in the afterlife; feelings are formed by experiences, opinions, and attitudes. The reaction to them may be extremely powerful and involuntary and may even create behaviour that is questionable and bizarre. One event demonstrating a positive emotion as a trigger was observed when children on a school trip visited a house built in the 1860s, now a museum to show what life was like in that era. The original owner had lost a grandchild in 1880. As the children entered the house, the entity saw a child who closely resembled her grandson. The resulting emotion triggered a physical manifestation and the woman appeared as a ghostly figure to the children. The feeling was not reciprocated and the children fled the house, screaming. One witness later stated that the apparition resembled an oil painting of the original owner, and the entire event lasted no more than a few seconds.

MY THOUGHTS ON THE MECHANICS OF MANIFESTATION

When an entity experiences a strong emotion, there is a shift within the electromagnetic field, causing it to polarize. When this dielectric field polarizes, it starts a chain reaction. There is an escalation in its normal operating frequency to a higher wavelength from 6.5 to 19 Hz. A harmonic resonance from within this field causes a wave to form from the memory matrix. This field begins absorption of materials and energy from within the surrounding environment. The absorbed materials become coherent and oscillate in harmony. This starts to produce the exact configuration of what the entity looked like in life, as demonstrated by the Kirlian effect as well as the DNA Phantom effect. UV wavelengths cause ion radiation that knocks electrons from atoms, causing them to become highly reactive, beginning the formulation of a lattice structure. This lattice vibrates in the infrasound spectrum at approximately 4 Hz.

As the material is pulled in from the proximity of the event, a thermal void develops within the area, leaving cold spots. A partial form may start to appear near room temperature or slightly above. Depending on its intensity, more of the form may be produced. If the emotional event is terminated, the manifestation will quickly dissipate. Depending on how long the manifestation maintains its form, the observation of auditory static discharge may be heard. Additionally, small pools of cold water may appear as condensation forms.

The amount of material collected from the surrounding environment will dictate the type of manifestation that occurs. Limited material may only allow a fog charged with ions. There may be light phenomena associated with this fog, due to the charged particles. Within low energy, long wave ultraviolet light photons may be captured by electrons, which are orbiting the nuclei of atoms. As they gain energy, they are boosted to excited states. As the electrons return to the lower energy state, there is a release of energy in the form of visible light. This light energy can be passed from one molecule to another.

Additional material will allow for more complex structures, ranging from a partial formation of the head and/or torso, right up to a solid body manifestation.

Depending on the structure and the ease with which information cascades within the structure (i.e. telekinesis, the true sense of the phrase "mind over matter"), this would allow for manipulation and would dictate the movements of the structure, as reported by witnesses. The movement may vary from a rigid form that seems to be unable to move, to what is termed a glider, right up to full animation.

THE MEMORY MATRIX, BUILDING A BUBBLE

The fabric that formulates a memory bubble is frequency resonating at a specific harmonic value. Each bubble has its own value. The bubble contains a slice of time, devised and perceived by the entity as reality. The time it represents is out of synch with real time.

Quantum physics explains that matter can be both a particle and a wave, and has proved that the same particle can appear in two places at the same time. In specific experiments, particles can react to the same stimulus at the same time, even though they are separated by great distances. There is still a great deal to learn, but say those distances were separated by time as well as space?

Example one: Ghosts have been observed as mist and shadows; this could be explained as a cloud of particles. Ghosts have also been seen as solid apparitions, so this could be a wave.

Example two: A house is haunted, and if it catches fire, is the ghost in danger?

No, its distance from the reality of the fire, even though it can perceive it, is vast. That distance is time. Its reality is both past and present. However, its default is in the past, so therefore in its time reality the house did not burn. The fire would be a future event that poses no threat to the inhabiting spirit. The house in the ghost's reality would remain as it always has, even if it were torn down and completely removed.

EXPLORATION OF THE GHOSTLY ATTRIBUTES

Let's look at some of the research. Electromagnetic energy exists within each of us. Science is now examining this energy at the cellular level, leading to the belief that it is a platform for communication from one cell to another. There is also ongoing research that is now trying to redefine what death is, as it has been discovered that, at the time of brain death, there remains communication within the body at the cellular level. Near-death researchers have regarded this with great interest, as subjects pronounced brain dead have reported actions and conversations within hospital emergency and operating rooms prior to resuscitation. Researchers now feel the information within the body was retained by this energy at the cellular level. Once the individual was revived, they had full knowledge of what had been going on while they were dead. This is very exciting on its own, but if we throw into the equation the fact that energy cannot be destroyed, could this information remain if the individual was not revived, and the individual body was pronounced dead?

It seems that when we do pass over, reality in some form continues. For the spirit, life seemingly goes on. These are the ones who do not know they are dead and believe everything is as it should be, but there are those who are quite aware they are dead. This became evident in some of the EVPs captured in our investigations. I find all electronic voice phenomena interesting, but where I really become fascinated is when we capture unsolicited comments about the environment, the team, or our equipment. In the Horse Palace Peter recorded an unseen person amongst the horse stalls saying, "You can't see me ... but I am here." It showed that he was well aware of us.

In the restaurant a male ghost recognized that Michele was psychic and didn't seem to appreciate her getting involved with him. As they came through a door, he said, "Thank you, cat witch bitch." In the archives a ghost perceived our equipment and warned another ghost not to cross its path, saying, "Laura ... camera." Regardless of our disadvantage, we captured incredible data by utilizing tested mediums and our limited technology, simply because we stayed the course and spent days and days hunting them.

ENERGY FIELDS AND WHAT THEY MIGHT MEAN

The U.S. military is very much aware of the energy within the human body and is conducting experiments to harness that power for operations in the field. This new type of field bio battery charging system is still in its infancy. The principle is that the human heart produces about four watts of energy as it pumps. This energy spirals like a flux around our bodies and produces a field that can extend up to fifteen feet beyond our bodies. Since the military wishes to harness this power to charge communication and GPS battery packs, it opens the window to some speculation. As this energy field moves around us, it has come into contact with other energy sources, energy fields, as demonstrated by the Kirlian Effect. Could this interaction allow transference of information, and can this media be associated with déjà vu, second sight, and empathic experiences? Most people have unlearned that method of processing this type of information, through fear, and have become deaf to the reception of such media. This explains gut feelings, which normally are a warning of sorts.

But does this energy truly retain information? In 1939, Semyon Kirlian discovered by accident what would eventually be termed the "Kirlian Effect," a photographic procedure that seems to capture the life force that surrounds every living thing. It was further noted in Kirlian investigations that changes in moisture could indicate emotional changes, which affect the coronal discharges around the subject. If these photos truly demonstrate the life force, then there would seem to be integrity within the memory matrix. This was demonstrated by his famous photo of a leaf that shows the top portion cut off and removed. The Kirlian photo shows the aura of the entire leaf. This seems to demonstrate that, even though the leaf is damaged and incomplete, there is something that remembers the integrity of the entire leaf, as displayed by the photo.

In 1985, at the Academy of Sciences in Moscow, a scientist was mapping a DNA sample with a laser. He had fired the laser into the target chamber but had forgotten to place his specimen slide into the target area. What occurred was an image of the previous DNA sample as though it was still present within the chamber, even though it had been removed. The equipment was inspected and further tests were conducted. They all produced the same result; it seemed the laser was being influenced by what is now termed "The DNA Phantom." It was determined that when the sample was removed, something remained, invisible to the human eye, that could influence light waves and leave an imprint. Can the energy signature of DNA leave a signature standing wave in its environment?

Could these invisible lines of force be part of the integrity of the Memory Matrix?

Special Note: In quantum physics, quantum coherence means that subatomic particles are able to co-operate with one another. Coherence establishes communication. Particles seem to be aware of each other and are connected by bands of electromagnetic fields. Let's imagine for a moment that they operate like a tuning fork and, as information cascades along these lines of electromagnetic fields, they all begin to resonate together. When this occurs, and they move into a phase synch, they all begin acting like one giant wave. It then becomes difficult to tell them apart. If some action is done to one of them, it will affect them all. It was discovered in 1923 by a Russian medical professor, Alexander G. Gurvich, that DNA is an essential source of light energy in the form of biophotons, or what he termed "mitogenetic rays." These rays exist in every living organism and operate in the ultraviolet spectrum of light. This may also be what produces the aura seen in the Kirlian effect. In this respect, DNA could then, in essence, be the master tuning fork, playing at a particular frequency, which starts a cascade of information, and all other particles fall in line and follow.

Ions are charged atoms. They can be negative (more electrons) or positive (more protons). A negative charge and a positive charge will attract each other, whereas two negatives or two positives will repel one another. Charged objects will create an electric field around themselves. Ions that become trapped will stay together and may produce a densely packed cloud. The ions within the cloud move by repelling and attracting one another. Ions can be generated in abundance whenever energy is transferred into the air. One method of transference is ultraviolet light. Positive ions can cause heavy, oppressed feelings.

The study of ions and static electricity has produced results that can be studied in a lab and reproduced. Results such as: hair standing on end, goose flesh, cold spots, and sensations of being touched. Furthermore, there can be various visual phenomena, such as glowing balls of light. Static discharge can produce snapping, crackling, and banging sounds, as well as water from condensation. All these phenomena have been reported in supposed hauntings.

I remember a particular Saturday night when I was conducting an investigation in the *Overshadows* project. I was walking down the hall on the upper floor. The activity in the house was abundant, and we were recording at the time. Something, or someone, came out of a room and ran towards me. On impact, it passed through me. My body felt as if it had just been woken up. I felt cold and tingly. Could this entity, having run through me, pulled hundreds, if not thousands of ions into me, causing this effect? Either way, what I thought meant very little; I had to prove it.

If we assemble some of the pieces and make a giant leap, we can ask ourselves what if something of us does survive after death, something that retains intelligence, emotion, and memory? What would it look like? Could it have some of the characteristics found in the above and exist as a small ball of invisibility, just beyond our perception? Could this be what Doctor Duncan MacDougall of Haverhill, Massachusetts, observed and reported in his experiments? He reported his death observation experiments in *American Medicine* in April of 1907. His subjects experienced at the time of death an unexplainable weight loss of between 1½ to 2½ ounces. Could this be something of the soul?

There seems to be several stages to what a ghost is in existence; they are invisible beyond our perception, stringy shadows, and some are a form of apparition. Let's start with the shadows and how and why we might see them. As I combed through hundreds of reports and articles, there seemed to be patterns and consistencies. First, I had to understand how the human eye works, which led me to a multitude of medical texts and several doctors and optometrists.

Every person has two types of vision: foveal, which is direct or focused vision, is our primary vision, since it is perfect for seeing details. The other is peripheral vision, which is suited for detecting and seeing shadows. Peripheral vision isn't used often, as we are no longer predators, hunting for our food and on guard against attacks from other predators. Our peripheral is designed to allow low-resolution vision, motion detection at 180 degrees at a wide range of illuminations. Foveal uses cones (colour vision), which have filters that prevent a large portion of ultraviolet (UV) light from reaching the retina. Peripheral uses rods (black and white vision), which are sensitive to ultraviolet light. In the majority of people the UV filters do not completely filter out all of the UV light, since there are small gaps at the corners of their eyes (peripheral).

WHY CHILDREN AND PETS PERCEIVE MORE PHENOMENA THAN ADULTS

The structure and development of the eye has a great deal to do with seeing ghosts. Spirit composition reflects UV light at certain points of the manifestation process; it is within the UV-A spectrum of 380 to 315 nanometers. It is the UV-A light that is the basis of the research, since UV-A is found both indoors and outdoors. UV-B 314–280nm and UV-C 279–200nm is not found indoors; the phenomenon is generally seen indoors.

The UV filters within the human eye develop over time, and with age the lens of the eye hardens and becomes yellow, thus allowing the eye to decrease its absorbing ability, blocking out more UV radiation with the exception of the peripheral. UV will enter the eyes of children and infants at full strength.

Dogs have the ability to detect movement in low lighting, and because of their short life span, they rarely develop the ability to block out UV light.

What does this have to do with ghosts? Let us examine several pieces of this puzzle.

An article appeared in the *Journal of the Society of Psychical Research*, regarding Mr. Vic Tandy and the Ghost in the Machine, Vol. 62, No. 851, April, 1998. It reported several instances of sensings and sightings of ghostly phenomena. Two important clues within the article are firstly, a standing wave Mr. Tandy discovered to be approximately 19 Hz, and secondly, all visual input related to the phenomena was always detected by the peripheral vision.

There are numerous reports of people relating the same phenomena, which are now being termed "Shadow People." This phenomenon is not new. People see black or dark image movement out of the peripheral, only to have it disappear when they turn their head. Is it possible that these shadow people exist in the UV spectrum of light? Or in better terms, they reflect UV light waves? When the observer turns to look directly at the image, does the UV filter within the eye instantly block it from our perception, and the image seems to have vanished?

This may be why monks in medieval times used small mirrors, placed up beside their noses, to see roaming spirits in their peripheral vision.

I began studying several photos of apparitions reflected in mirrors. The photos didn't show an apparition in the room, but the reflection clearly showed an image within the mirror. Because in-depth experiments with infrared imaging proved to be extremely poor, I started to look at the other end of visible light, ultraviolet light. This seemed exciting, because very little research and exploration has been conducted in the UV spectrum. The camera flash, when fired, not only flared visible light, but also UV light. I believe it was the UV flare that, when impacting and interacting with a spirit's energy signature passing through this field, left a split-second imprint upon a mirror or reflective surface, and, acting like the emulsions of film, lasted long enough for the camera to capture the image. This produced a photo image, not of the spirit, but of a reflection of the spirit. After I discussed with John Mullan much of my theory on UV waves and their relationship with spirit energy, he summed it up with an analogy. "It is like dust particles floating around the room, you can't see them, but regardless they are still there. It's when you catch a sunbeam shining in through a window — the floating dust is suddenly illuminated."

It was further noted on our surveillance tapes from a haunted house in Toronto we worked in a few years ago that although there were sounds in the hallway right in front of the camera, nothing could be seen directly. However, when the sun peeked in the front room window, there was an immediate reaction, and images began to appear. Because we couldn't see in the UV light spectrum, we could not determine exactly what was going on. What we did see were unusual light phenomena, such as light bending around corners, bowing in certain areas, pulsating and not producing a consistent saturation within the field of view. We further observed a strange fog that interplayed with the light, sometimes mingling with it, sometimes pushing it back in spots. Images can be seen within the light and fog, although not clearly. There are also times when the sunlight is clearly coming in the front window, while a stronger light comes from the opposite direction, pushing the sunlight back out of the hallway.

THE MEMORY MATRIX AND THE PING-PONG BALL

One evening at the house investigated in the book *Overshadows*, my wife and I had gone over to visit the family when a strange event occurred. Over the course of our visit, the daughter of the family suggested we play ping-pong. Everyone agreed, feeling that a little bit of fun would be a good stress relief from the events normally occurring in the house. During the game, a wild return of the ball left the table and struck something in open space, something we couldn't see. The ball ricocheted back and forth in what seemed to be a very tight space. After bouncing about ten to twelve times in rapid succession, the ball fell to the floor. It was witnessed by all five of us.

NO NAKED GHOSTS

A memory bubble is a reality created by an individual spirit, in which it exists. The bubble matrix consists of a period in time and space, familiar to the individual when they were living. It has been discovered that in near-death experiences, there are constant common events. The first is a noise, like a buzzing, which actually could be the change in frequency from this reality to the next reality. All report that they lose track of time; it has little meaning to them. They enter a life review. This review normally follows a chronology, from birth to the point of death. It is in the near-death experience that these people are turned back. Had they not been resuscitated, I believe the individual would have chosen a slice of time from their life review, and that time frame would have then become their new reality. Their reality contains all the things that one would find in this reality, such as sight, sound, furniture, and people, living and deceased, and because the mental attributes are intact, they also retain humility, which is why naked ghosts are rarely seen. The phrase "My life flashed before my eyes" is an appropriate statement within this context. At the point of death, an individual's life will, out of memory, replay itself. This process can last up to three days and is part of the memory bubble development. The deceased will eventually select a point in time from their memory. Once selected, they will choose to exist within that memory. This selection will, of course, have a deep personal meaning.

The modification and expansion of a memory bubble occurs when more than one spirit in close proximity share a specific time frame. One example would be where many people died in a single event such as war. They rely on each other's memory information of that time and adapt the information to the bubble, causing it to expand.

The bubble appears to produce a narrow field time shift. This bubble envelops them and moves with them. However, if this cluster contains many entities, the bubble grows as well. In some cases it can extend beyond the group, and it is possible for someone living to pass into and through this bubble, thus experiencing a time shift.

For example, in 1901 there was a case involving two English women, Miss Anne Moberley and Miss Eleanor Jourdain, who, on a trip to Paris, reported that while walking the grounds of Versailles, they seemed to walk into the past. They saw people in period dress from the late eighteenth century, around the time of the Revolution, and reported that the environment around them had changed, feeling heavy, depressed, and very unpleasant.

It's within this bubble that a spirit's thought process, if traumatic and powerful, may manifest into our reality, and should it be reinforced with those of other spirits, it could take on a life of its own. The manifestation can separate from the memory bubble and form its own reality. This would explain the sightings of ghostly ships and trains, most of which suffered some devastating fate in history. That manifestation bubble which has detached and is not supported seems real, but it quickly dissipates without warning and is gone from the witness's view.

HOW A LIVING INDIVIDUAL AND A SPIRIT MEET AT A POINT WITHIN TIME AND SPACE

The spirit is outside of our perception, existing within its memory bubble. Occasionally something occurs that serves as a switch to synchronization of the two realities, allowing them to collide in time and space. The best way to explain this is, if you remember having a dream where a sound around you, possibly a clock radio going off, was incorporated into your dream, and instead of waking you up, it changed your dream and became a part of it. This will give you a better understanding of what is taking place. The synchronicity occurs when the spirit memory perceives a living individual as part of their memory bubble, due to a resemblance or out of simple convenience, causing the spirit to come forward to interact and emotions to escalate. It is at this point of interaction that the two realities collide. The living individual becomes terrified, and the spirit, realizing this person is not part of their reality, quickly retreats back beyond our perception.

WHAT MEMORY MATRIX DEVELOPMENT REPRESENTS AND WHAT IT MEANS WITH REGARD TO JUDGMENT DAY.

I never wanted to fall into a discussion of religion, because I understand that this can be an extremely delicate subject. Everyone has, or should have, the freedom to follow and practice the religion of their choice. Regardless of the religion, they all have the same principle messages for all of us.

1. Be good to one another; take care of those around us.
2. Believe in and worship God.

Now, having said that, I have to tread into the deeper water of what all religions consider a Day of Judgment. There are commonalities between Judeo-Christian and Islamic teachings. The top of the list is that they agree there will be such a day.

The memory bubble is developed out of the individual's memory, consisting of events, emotions, and experience.

People are, believe it or not, their own harshest critics and they will, without knowing, put themselves where they need to be. People are creatures of habit, and through that habit will take all of life's events, emotions, and experiences with them into death, involuntarily becoming what they have always been in life. They will unknowingly choose an interim place of existence.

Heaven

The individual has died, accepted, and acknowledged their sins in life and found an enjoyable place in time where they were most happy. The memory bubble is then formed around that time, transferring them to an existence of peaceful harmony. These entities are quiet.

Hell

The individual has died and is obsessed with things they have done, or that had been done to them; over money, property, or a relationship. They are trying to make people understand that they were a victim or are continuing to hide a crime. They virtually transform themselves into an undying hell, where the memory bubble they create contains all the sins and fears that haunted them in life. These entities are restless and active. Some may be malevolent, some benevolent.

These two places are temporary until the final Day of Judgment, where all will be collected and brought forth, along with the living, for Judgment.

It wasn't long ago (1999) that Pope John Paul II spoke to an audience in Rome about the nature of Heaven and Hell. He stated that neither was a physical place, but rather what the individual made of them; they are more states of thought.

—/—

I don't profess to know the secrets of life after death, but rather through observation, research, and experimentation have put together what I believe to be true. I have great hope that paranormal investigators and researchers will give what I have written at least some of their consideration and work with it. Maybe together, in time, we can solve this great mystery.

Also by Richard Palmisano

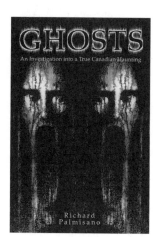

Ghosts
An Investigation into a True Canadian Haunting

$22.99

978-1554884353

This amazing true story is a frightening account of a three year investigation into the multiple haunting of a once-grand Mississauga mansion on the shores of Lake Ontario. During the day, this remarkable place with its rolling green lawns is like a dream come true. But the dream turns into a nightmare as the sun goes down. When darkness falls, the overwhelming feeling of being watched takes over. Things move here, shadows swirl around you, spirits whisper to themselves.

Join renowned paranormal investigator, Richard Palmisano and his team, the Searcher Group, as the spirits at the lakeshore mansion lead them to the terrible secrets hidden inside the grounds and an encounter with a ghost full of anger and hate. In this chilling story, spirits interact with one another in an attempt to protect themselves from the intruders. Find out how far they are willing to go to get the investigators to leave and never come back!

Overshadows

An Investigation into a Terrifying Modern Canadian Haunting

$19.99

978-1550024739

In 1995, a young girl living with her abusive mother committed suicide. Shortly afterwards, her spirit returned to the house, only to find her mother gone and strangers moving in. She also found the older spirits who dwell there, beginning a powerful battle for control of the house — and trapping its new residents in the middle.

Overshadows chronicles the events of this terrifying multiple haunting, but more importantly, it shares the incredible discoveries made during the course of a six-year investigation. This book will challenge and disprove classic theories, and create upheaval in the circle of life-after-death research.

Available at your favourite bookseller.

www.dundurn.com

What did you think of this book?
Visit www.dundurn.com for reviews, videos, updates, and more!